One-Pot Cooking

ONE~POT COOKING

Pamela Westland

ELM TREE BOOKS · LONDON

First published in Great Britain 1978
by Elm Tree Books/Hamish Hamilton Ltd
90 Great Russell Street London WC1B 3PT

Photographs by Studio Lorenzini
Illustrations by Dick Barnard

The publishers gratefully acknowledge the assistance
of Thorn Domestic Appliances, manufacturers of the
Kenwood cook pots and cook pans seen in the
photographs in this book.

H.B. breakfast china from Quimper, Brittany,
courtesy of Liberty & Co. Ltd, Regent Street,
London W1.

Hand-made pottery from a selection at Six Apples,
Wethersfield, Braintree, Essex.

Peter Piper pepper mills and fluted baking dishes from
Etcetera, 15 Market Place, Great Dunmow, Essex.

Mushrooms supplied by Blue Prince Mushrooms

British Library Cataloguing in Publication Data
Westland, Pamela
    One-pot cooking.
    1. Cookery
    I. Title
    641.5'89   TX840.S/
    ISBN 0-241-89599-5

Filmset and printed in Great Britain by
BAS Printers Limited, Over Wallop, Hampshire

Contents

A note on the measurements

Ingredients have been listed in both metric and imperial (in brackets) measures. It is most important to follow one set of measurements or the other, as they are not exact conversions. Liquid measures actually convert at $\frac{1}{2}$ pint $= 280$ ml and 1 pint $= 560$ ml; these have been rounded up in all cases to 300 and 600 ml.

Introduction

One-pot cooking is not a new idea, it is a very old one. But cooking methods, like so many other things, seem to go in cycles. From the earliest times through the period when ovens were a luxury enjoyed by very few, all cooking was done over an open fire, and meat was either roasted on a make-shift spit or boiled in a pot hanging over the embers. There was only space for a single pot, and so everything went into it: a piece of fat pork, perhaps a rabbit, hare or old hen, a bunch of pot herbs—onions, garlic, leeks, cabbage, celery and carrots—and a suet pudding wrapped in a cloth and suspended in the simmering broth. A rack might be put across the pot and small vessels stood on it, to cook potted meats, fruit compôte or porridge. And of course the broth itself would make many a nourishing bowl of soup. In most households, it was a luxury to send a piece of meat, a cake or pie to the baker's to cook in his oven when the day's batch of bread was done.

The most recent English way of cooking a dinner—a piece of meat and at least two vegetables separately, on different gas or electric rings—costs money, and makes us stop to think. Fuel is expensive not only in terms of the household budget but in the wider sense of the national economy. And so we have come almost full circle, not right back to the multi-storey cooking in a single pot, but to examining all the different means by which we can cook rich, nourishing meals in one pot, using only a single source of heat.

One-pot cooking saves money first and foremost; but that is not its only advantage. Think of the joy, after a relaxing meal with family and friends, of having only a single pot to wash up, instead of a roasting pan and three saucepans. Think of the vitamins all preserved in the stock or sauce, instead of being thrown thoughtlessly away with the vegetable water. And think of the cheaper cuts of meat which adapt miraculously to long, slow cooking methods. This is one way of taking a slash at rising prices, and making sure of getting true value for your money.

The actual method you use to follow the recipes will depend on the appliances you have and the amount of time at your disposal. If you come in from a busy day at the office or in the shops and you have not had time to prepare a meal in advance, the speed of a pressure cooker will be a positive

God-send. If, on the other hand, you have been able to spare a little time to make the initial preparations the night before and want to spend a long day away from home, then the long, slow and sure cooking an electric cook pot offers you will be ideal.

The methods I have given are the ones I have found to produce the best balance of tenderness, colour and flavour. They do not all say just take the lid off the appliance, tip the ingredients in, replace the lid and apply the heat—though you can do this with some. Many of the recipes recommend that all or some of the ingredients are gently fried in butter or oil first, to take away the 'raw' flavour of onion or garlic, and to seal the flavour into the meat; otherwise it escapes into the sauce. If you are using a flameproof casserole, an electric cook pan or a pressure cooker, you can carry out this initial 'browning' of the ingredients, stir in the stock and continue cooking all in the same vessel. Without one of these appliances—if you want to use an ovenproof casserole or an electric slow cooker, for instance—you might choose to brown the ingredients in a frying pan first, then transfer them to the casserole. Or not bother to brown them at all. It is up to you.

There is another counsel of perfection in the matter of adding stock to vegetables and meat after a little flour has been stirred in. Undoubtedly stock that you have heated first, to the temperature of the ingredients in the pan, blends in more readily and gives a smoother sauce. But it means another pan, and there will probably be times when you will not think it worth it.

The cooking temperatures and times given in the recipes are oven temperatures and times taken in the oven or on top of the stove, as stated, in an ordinary flameproof casserole. Most of the recipes can easily be adapted to other appliances, and in every instance I have indicated which appliances would be suitable. When using one of these, remember to follow the manufacturer's instructions in the leaflet concerned. Even a similar type of appliance varies in the heat output from one maker to another. Follow the directions for the particular one you have and you cannot go wrong.

Electric cook pans

You will see that a very high proportion of the recipes are marked as suitable for electric cook pans. These appliances really are amazingly versatile—and not to be confused with electric frying pans. The cook pans can be used for roasting, braising, frying, stewing, boiling and steaming—in fact, there is scarcely any cooking they cannot manage, only grilling! When I was moving house recently and was without a cooker for a few weeks, I cooked for ourselves and for hordes of visitors entirely in an electric cook pan and electric slow cooker, and I don't think anyone guessed. I blanch vegetables for the freezer in the pan—it is a wonderfully quick source of heat, and has a large capacity—and use it now for making all my preserves. And I wouldn't dream of lighting the oven to cook a small family meal when it's so much cheaper to use the cook pan. Recipes suitable for cooking in this way are marked with a ⬛ and, as I said, you will see that there are a great many of them.

Electric slow cookers

Here is an appliance that I feel sure my grandmother would have loved to have had in her kitchen. She would have approved of the slow, even heat, the economy you can almost see, and of course the reassurance that food positively cannot spoil. Electric slow cookers are a relatively new appliance on the market. They are new to the manufacturers, too, and although they are already excellent I suppose that more and more modifications and improvements will be made to them in time. For example, they will probably soon be able to reach an initial temperature high enough to brown meat and vegetables before the long, slow cooking process commences. Most manufacturers recommend that you switch the appliance to the higher heat for the first part of the cooking time, and then, if you wish, to the lower one to complete the meal. At present there is only one model available with an automatic switch-over, so that this can take place in your absence, by thermostatic control. But this is not to say that these pots are not already a masterpiece of ingenuity and have revolutionised the cooking of a great many working wives and mothers. With a meal cooking slowly and surely all day long, ready when you and the family arrive home, that dreadful rush, tear and scramble to prepare a meal in the evening is eliminated once and for all. It is up to you whether you put in all the ingredients at once, or whether you decide to fry them in a separate pan before transferring them to the slow cooker. This largely depends on the importance to you, at the time, of having an extra pan to wash; whether you want the meal to start as well as finish all in one pot. All the recipes marked ⬛ have been tested in at least one of two cook pots; one has a separate lift-out casserole which fits inside the heated casing and the other is all in one piece. Because these appliances are a whole new way of cooking, and the different models reach varying degrees of high temperature, always check your manufacturer's instructions before adapting a recipe. Check, too, that the following table of the cooking times for one of these pots conforms in general—whether the meat is cut in pieces or in a whole joint—with your own recipe leaflet.

General Guide to Cooking Times for Electric Slow Cookers

Food	Slow Cooking	Extra Slow Cooking
Beef, whole (0·9–1·35 kg/ 2–3 lb)	High 3½–4 hrs	
Beef, cubed	High 4 hrs	High 2 hrs, then low 8 hrs
Chicken, whole (0·9–1·35 kg/2–3 lb)	High 4 hrs	

Food	Slow Cooking	Extra Slow Cooking
Chicken, joints	High 3½ hrs	High 2 hrs, then low 7 hrs
Chicken, cubed	High 3 hrs	High 2 hrs, then low 6 hrs
Gammon (450–900 g/		
1–2 lb)	High 4 hrs	
0·9–1·35 kg—2–3 lb)	High 5 hrs	
Pork, cubed	High 4 hrs	High 2 hrs, then low 8 hrs
Rabbit, whole	High 3½–4 hrs	High 2 hrs, then low 7–8 hrs
Rabbit, joints	High 3½ hrs	High 2 hrs, then low 7 hrs
Rabbit, cubed	High 3 hrs	High 2 hrs, then low 6 hrs
Veal, cubed	High 4 hrs	High 2 hrs, then low 8 hrs
*Beans, butter	High 4–5 hrs	
*Beans, haricot	High 4–6 hrs	High 2 hrs, then low 8–10 hrs
*Beans, kidney	High 4–5 hrs	High 2 hrs, then low 7–8 hrs
*Carrots, whole or thickly sliced	High 4–6 hrs	High 2 hrs, then low 8–12 hrs
*Carrots, diced or thinly sliced	High 3–5 hrs	High 2 hrs, then low 6–12 hrs
*Celery, chopped or sliced	High 3–6 hrs	High 2 hrs, then low 6–12 hrs
*Leeks, sliced	High 3–5 hrs	High 2 hrs, then low 6–10 hrs
*Lentils, small	High 1–2 hrs	High 2 hrs, then low 3–6 hrs
*Lentils, large	High 2–3 hrs	High 2 hrs, then low 6 hrs
*Mushrooms	High 3–8 hrs	High 2 hrs, then low 6–10 hrs
*Potatoes, whole or thickly sliced	High 4–6 hrs	High 2 hrs, then low 8–12 hrs
*Potatoes, diced or thinly sliced	High 3–5 hrs	High 2 hrs, then low 6–12 hrs
*Swedes, whole or thickly sliced	High 4–6 hrs	High 2 hrs, then low 8–12 hrs
*Swedes, diced or thinly sliced	High 3–5 hrs	High 2 hrs, then low 6–12 hrs
*Turnips, whole or thickly sliced	High 4–6 hrs	High 2 hrs, then low 8–12 hrs
*Turnips, diced or thinly sliced	High 3–5 hrs	High 2 hrs, then low 8–12 hrs

*These ingredients have been given a range of times so that they can be interchanged with various meats. Due to the nature of the slow-cooking process, the ingredients will be cooked by the shortest time given, and will remain in similar state—without overcooking—until the maximum time given.

Pressure cookers

I think it is true to say that pressure cooking was a little in recession for a few years; at least, I certainly knew several people, including myself, who had a pressure cooker at the back of a cupboard, but had practically forgotten how to use it. And then the fuel crisis came, the cost of fuel soared, and anyway time became more and more precious. Practically every recipe in the book is suitable for cooking by this method. Only those with the longest cooking times, and therefore the biggest potential savings, are marked 🍲.But if you are a pressure-cooker addict, as so many of us have learned to be recently, you will doubtless use yours more and more.

In a sense, pressure cookers are the closest of all to the old idea of one-pot cooking—the meat, vegetables and other items all in a single pot. For with a meat and vegetable dish in the base of the pot and a trivet above it with vegetables in the separate containers, you can have a whole meal ready at the same time, yet ensure that each ingredient retains its own individuality. Pressure cookers do, of course, give you the opportunity to fry some of the ingredients first, then add the stock and other vegetables. And they give you the winter warming luxury of a steamed meat or fruit pudding in a fraction of the conventional cooking time.

Flameproof casseroles

Flameproof casseroles seem to me to have great advantages, for this type of cooking, over those which are simply ovenproof; and on no account must we confuse the two! You can carry out the initial browning–cooking stages, put the casserole into the oven for the long, slow part of the process, and then bring it to the top of the stove to raise the temperature again for the addition, perhaps, of a handful of dumplings. Most of the recipes which follow are suitable for flameproof casseroles; but long, slow cooking in the oven uses fuel, and so it is worth considering the other methods indicated with the recipes.

Hay boxes

For generations people have known that cooking can continue in a covered pot without any further source of heat at all. And so if you bring a casserole to simmering point, all you have to do is to maintain that temperature and the cooking process will continue—free. You can do this in a very make-shift way, in a cardboard box insulated with old newspapers, blankets or hay—or a mixture of all three. Or you can buy one of the new insulated devices designed specifically for the job. I have tested one which looks like a large red pouffe, all soft and cushiony. You simply put the pot, simmering and with a tightly fitting lid, into the centre, wrap a series of long padded strips and cushions around it, and leave it to cook—without being tempted to peep and see how it is getting on. I have not marked any specific recipes as suitable for hay boxes or vacuum flasks (below)—but almost all the soups can finish cooking in either of these, and stews and casseroles are ideal for hay-box cooking. Experiment with these methods and you're sure to save money.

Vacuum flasks

Vacuum flasks can continue the cooking process, too—in exactly the same way. Indeed, there can scarcely be a better way to carry hot food to a picnic, or on a long, cold fishing trip than in a wide-necked vacuum flask or jug. If food is simmering hot when you put it in, it will be just as hot, and a great deal more tender and succulent, when it is time to serve it.

Oven bricks

Some years ago, I bought what was described as a 'chicken brick' in order to get as close as I could to the original method of cooking Tandoori chicken. I couldn't see myself burying a clay pot up to its neck in the garden and lighting a charcoal fire in it, but I did achieve some mouth-watering results in the chicken brick. Not only chicken, but all other kinds of joints take perfectly to this method of cooking. Chicken and duck cook with skin as crisp as can be; the crackling on pork is crunchy hard; and rack of lamb—a favourite of mine—cooks to an unbelievable tenderness. Again, follow the directions that come with the brick when you use it for any of these recipes. The food is cooked for a relatively short time at a very high heat. In an ordinary roasting tin it would burn, but in an oven brick it doesn't.

When I tested these recipes, I made larger quantities than those I have given here, froze some and experimented with different fillings, toppings, stuffings, sauces. And so one basic casserole, prepared in the batch-baking principle, came to the table in numerous different ways, but always in one pot. I found this the most economical way of working on the recipes for testing purposes, and I still find it the most economical for ordinary family living. I hope you will too.

WHAT'S FOR BREAKFAST?

I'm hopeless in the mornings. A real sleepwalker until the third cup of coffee. And the very worst candidate, therefore, to play the gracious hostess to overnight guests. How they must long to come downstairs and find breakfast, tempting and delicious, ready on the sideboard. And so do I!

The very first time I made an effort to overcome this difficulty, and made the porridge overnight, it was like having a kitchen full of servants, below stairs. I simply brought the porridge (with plenty of salt in it) to simmering point, put it in a covered casserole and left it in the lower oven of my solid-fuel cooker. It was heaven to have at least one course steaming hot and waiting! You can put the porridge in a wide-necked vacuum flask, too, and it goes on 'cooking' beautifully for hours. I have also put porridge, and lots of other dishes, in a modern version of a hay box—like a big cushion pouffe. It works like a dream.

There aren't too many slow-cooking breakfast dishes that can simmer away while you slumber. But there are a great number that can be prepared in advance right up to the grilling or baking stage. The recipes in this section are taken from those I have come to rely on when people are staying. Some of them are not, strictly speaking, one-pot, but if you prepare everything in advance, you will need to worry about only one pot at breakfast time. And I'd far rather spend twenty minutes in the kitchen by myself the night before than try to juggle with two frying pans and a coffee pot while everyone fights over the morning paper.

Bacon and eggs are traditional for breakfast, of course, but it's fun to ring the changes and present them in new, one-pot ways—and it's usually cheaper, too. Cheese, so popular first thing in the morning in many European countries, makes sense in this context. It's a perfect instant nutritious food—packed with the kind of energy people need to get up and run for the bus! With only a little more indulgence, the addition, perhaps, of grilled tomatoes or mushrooms, or a salad, many of these ideas would carry on well to brunch. Two meals for the price—and effort—of one!

Cheese Gnocchi

You can prepare these semolina-paste triangles the night before, leaving them all ready, with the halved tomatoes, to be baked in the morning.

300 ml (½ pint) chicken stock (see page 24)
300 ml (½ pint) milk
100 g (4 oz) semolina
50 g (2 oz) grated cheese

salt and freshly-ground black pepper
8 large tomatoes, halved
mixed dried herbs

Put the chicken stock and milk together in a pan and bring it just to boiling point. Remove from the heat and sprinkle on the semolina. Beat immediately with a wooden spoon, return to the heat and simmer, stirring, until the mixture thickens. Turn on to a well-greased baking sheet (I use a non-stick swiss roll tin) and leave to set. Cut the paste into triangles and return them to the baking sheet. Sprinkle them with grated cheese and pepper. Cut the tomatoes in half, put them on the baking sheet and sprinkle them with salt, pepper and herbs. You can prepare the meal to this stage the day before, and refrigerate it overnight.

Bake the gnocchi and tomatoes at 200°C (400°F)/Gas 6 for 15 minutes, when they should be golden brown and bubbly.

Serves 4

Welsh Griddle Scones

If you are baking at tea-time, make and cut out a batch of savoury griddle scones, ready to cook for breakfast.

225 g (8 oz) flour
3 teaspoons baking powder
½ teaspoon mustard powder
½ teaspoon salt
freshly-ground black pepper
50 g (2 oz) margarine

25 g (1 oz) cooked ham, finely chopped
1 tablespoon fresh chopped parsley
about 150 ml (¼ pint) milk

Sieve the flour, baking powder, mustard, salt and pepper into a bowl. Rub in the margarine and stir in the ham and parsley. Mix with enough milk to form a soft but firm dough. Roll out on a floured board to a thickness of 1 cm (½ in). Cut into 7·5-cm (3-in) squares, then triangles.

Grease a large frying pan or griddle iron and heat it. Cook the scones over a high heat for 12–15 minutes, turning them once, until they are springy, and golden brown on both sides. Serve hot with butter.

Serves 6

3

Potato Scones

I used to make these when there was a bread shortage, to serve hot with peanut butter or honey. For a more substantial and traditional breakfast, you can cook bacon rashers on a baking sheet, or in the cook pan, beside them.

450 g (1 lb) potatoes, boiled   *½ teaspoon salt*
25 g (1 oz) butter   *freshly-ground black pepper*
a little milk   *100 g (4 oz) flour*

Mash the potatoes with butter, add a little milk and season well. Knead in the flour and continue kneading until the mixture is smooth. Roll out on a lightly-floured board to 1 cm (½ in) thick and cut into triangles. Place on a well-greased baking sheet and cook at 240°C (475°F)/Gas 9 for 10 minutes, flipping the scones over at half time. Serve hot, in a serving dish lined with a cotton napkin.

Serves 4

Curd Pancakes

Fat little pancakes are sandwiched together in this recipe with a curd cheese filling.

For the filling: For the pancakes:
225 g (8 oz) curd cheese   *100 g (4 oz) self-raising flour*
100 g (4 oz) ham, cooked and   *½ teaspoon salt*
chopped   *1 egg*
50 g (2 oz) mushrooms, cooked and *300 ml (½ pint) milk*
chopped   *cooking oil to fry*
1 teaspoon mustard powder
2 gherkins, finely chopped
salt and freshly-ground black pepper

To make the filling, just mix all the ingredients together in a small bowl and season well with salt and pepper. Leave covered overnight.

For the pancakes, sieve the flour and salt into a bowl, make a well in the centre and drop in the egg. Gradually add the milk, beating well until the batter is smooth. Leave the batter to stand.

Heat a little cooking oil in a large frying pan and drop in spoonfuls of the batter. Flip the pancakes over to brown the second side. Serve hot, sandwiched together with a thick layer of curd filling.

Serves 6

Rich Drop Scones

This old Welsh recipe thoughtfully instructs that the batter should be left to stand overnight, to 'settle'—what better for a breakfast treat?

100 g (4 oz) self-raising flour
pinch of salt
50 g (2 oz) butter
25 g (1 oz) sugar

2 eggs, beaten
150 ml (¼ pint) buttermilk or milk
cooking oil

Sift the flour and salt together into a bowl, rub in the butter and stir in the sugar. Add the beaten eggs and milk gradually, beating well to make a smooth batter. Leave to stand.

Lightly oil a heavy frying pan or griddle iron. When the surface is hot, drop the mixture on with a spoon and cook over a high heat until the top bubbles and the underside is golden brown, too. Keep the first scones hot by wrapping them in a clean tea towel while you cook the others. Serve hot with butter and ginger marmalade.

Serves 4

Frittered Apples

A sweet and crisp welcome to the day, slices of apple frizzed up in batter.

100 g (4 oz) flour
pinch of salt
¼ teaspoon ground cinnamon
4 eggs

4 eating apples, cored and thinly
sliced
40 g (1½ oz) lard for frying
caster sugar to decorate

Put the flour, salt and cinnamon into a bowl, add the eggs and whisk well until smooth and creamy. Mix in the apple slices. Heat the lard in a frying pan over a moderately high heat and drop in spoonfuls of the mixture. Fry for 1–2 minutes on each side, until crisp and golden brown. Drain on kitchen paper and serve hot, dredged with caster sugar.

Serves 4

Marmalade Soufflé Omelette

Not the kind of recipe for mornings when the school bus is due any second, but elegant enough to stand up to a special occasion.

For each person:
2 eggs, separated
1 dessertspoon caster sugar
2 teaspoons water

15 g (½ oz) butter
2 tablespoons marmalade, warmed
icing sugar, sifted, to decorate

Put an omelette pan on a low heat. Whisk together the egg yolks, sugar and water until pale and creamy. Whisk the egg whites and fold them into the mixture with a metal spoon. Melt the butter in the pan, pour in the omelette mixture and spread evenly with a knife. Cook, without moving the pan, until the bottom is set and a pale golden brown. Flash the top under a hot grill for about ½ minute. Spread the marmalade across the centre of the omelette and slide on to a warm plate, flipping the omelette to fold it in half. Dust the top with icing sugar. When the last member of the family is served, enjoy your own while someone else copes with the coffee.

Serves 1

Fish Kebabs *(photograph facing page 36)*

Fish for breakfast—marinated overnight, threaded on skewers all ready to pop under the grill in the morning.

450 g (1 lb) cod fillet, skinned	For the marinade:
4 rashers streaky bacon, without	*2 tablespoons cooking oil*
rind, cut in half	*4 tablespoons clear honey*
2 small onions, peeled	*3 tablespoons cider vinegar*
50 g (2 oz) button mushrooms,	*1 tablespoon lemon juice, strained*
wiped	*¼ teaspoon mixed dried herbs*
8 small tomatoes, halved	*1 tablespoon fresh chopped parsley*

Brush 4 skewers with oil. Cut the fish into even cubes. Roll the bacon up into coils, halve the onions and divide them into sections, halve the mushrooms if they are large. Thread the fish, bacon, onions, mushrooms and tomatoes on the skewers so that they alternate for flavour and colour.

Mix the marinade ingredients in a small bowl. Lay the threaded skewers on a shallow dish and pour over the marinade. Turn the skewers from time to time and leave them overnight.

Line the grill rack with household foil. Grill the kebabs under a moderate heat for 15 minutes, brushing with the marinade and turning the skewers frequently. Serve with hot, buttered toast.

Serves 4

Bornholm Omelette

Omelettes make sense for breakfast. They seem to me less complicated than cooking eggs and all the other ingredients separately. This idea, from Denmark, is tasty and quick.

*1 200-g (7-oz) can herring fillets,
    drained*
8 eggs
2 tablespoons single cream

*salt and freshly-ground black
    pepper*
40 g (1½ oz) butter

Cut the herring fillets into strips. Beat together the eggs, cream, salt and pepper. Melt the butter in a large omelette pan or electric cook pan, pour in the egg mixture and cook slowly, shaking the pan to cook evenly. When the mixture has set, slide the omelette on to a heated serving plate. Arrange the herring fillets on top and put under a moderate grill for about 2 minutes to warm the fish through. Serve in wedges with hot, buttered toast.

Serves 4

Sardine Omelette

The same, only different. Canned fish is invaluable for quick breakfast meals, and combines perfectly with eggs.

25 g (1 oz) butter
*1 small onion, peeled and finely
    chopped*
*225 g (8 oz) potato, boiled and
    diced*
6 eggs

salt and freshly-ground black pepper
¼ teaspoon mixed dried herbs
1 can sardines in tomato sauce

Heat the butter in a large omelette pan, add the onion and cook until soft but not brown. Mix in the potato and fry for 2–3 minutes. Beat the eggs with the salt, pepper and herbs and pour into the pan. Stir lightly from the sides of the pan. When the eggs are set, arrange the sardines in a wheel formation. Put the pan under a heated grill just to warm the fish. Serve straight from the pan, in wedges, with hot, buttered toast.

Serves 4

Haddock Scramble

One small finnan haddock serves four when it's tumbled into scrambled eggs.

1 small finnan haddock, cooked
50 g (2 oz) butter
8 eggs
pinch of cayenne pepper

grated rind of ½ lemon
1 tablespoon fresh chopped parsley
1 tablespoon cream
4 slices hot, buttered toast

Skin, bone and flake the haddock. Melt the butter in a pan and heat the haddock. Beat the eggs lightly with the pepper, lemon rind and chopped parsley. Pour on to the haddock and cook over a low heat, stirring occasionally, until just set. Stir in the cream and serve at once on the hot, buttered toast.

Serves 4

Fishcakes

My husband positively insisted I include a fishcake recipe—so that he was sure to have them when I cooked a batch to test.

25 g (1 oz) butter
25 g (1 oz) flour
150 ml (¼ pint) milk, warm
cayenne pepper
few drops of red pepper sauce
175 g (6 oz) smoked haddock,
  cooked

1 egg, beaten
toasted breadcrumbs
fat for frying
curry powder to serve
parsley sprigs to garnish

Melt the butter in a pan, add the flour and stir to make a roux. Gradually pour on the warm milk and stir until the sauce boils and thickens. Remove from the heat and season with a good pinch of cayenne pepper and a few drops of pepper sauce. Remove the skin and bones and flake the fish. Stir it into the sauce, then spread the mixture on a plate to cool. Flour your hands and shape the mixture into 8 rounds. Toss them in beaten egg and then in the toasted crumbs until they are completely coated. You can prepare the fishcakes to this stage the day before, and refrigerate them overnight. Heat the fat in a frying pan and fry the fishcakes, turning them once, until golden brown on both sides. Sprinkle with a little curry powder and garnish with parsley.

Serves 4

Bacon Kebabs *(photograph facing page 36)*

Often it's cheaper to buy a small piece of bacon than rashers. This is a good, unusual breakfast way of serving it.

675 g (1½ lb) bacon slipper or
  forehock, or use 325 g (¾ lb) bacon
  rashers, de-rinded and rolled
3 large bananas
2 small onions, peeled and halved

50 g (2 oz) butter, melted
8 small tomatoes
freshly-ground black pepper
demerara sugar

Remove the rind and fat from the bacon and cut it into 2-cm ($\frac{3}{4}$-in) cubes. Simmer them in water for 25 minutes, then drain. (You can do this the night before; if you're using bacon rashers, there's no need to simmer them.) Peel the bananas and cut them on a diagonal into strips. Separate the onion halves into sections. Brush 4 skewers with some of the melted butter and thread alternately the bacon cubes, banana slices, onion pieces and tomatoes on to the skewers. Season well with pepper and sprinkle with a little demerara sugar. Brush with more melted butter and place under a hot grill for 8 minutes, turning the skewers and brushing them with the remaining butter from time to time.

Serves 4

Sausage Kebabs *(photograph facing page 36)*

Assemble the kebabs the night before, and all you will have to do in the morning is put them under the grill while everyone's eating their cereal.

12 chipolata sausages
German mustard
8 button mushrooms, wiped
2 onions, peeled and halved
cooking oil

1 green pepper, trimmed and cut into squares
salt and freshly-ground black pepper

Cut the sausages into small wedges and cut each wedge lengthwise. Spread the pieces generously with mustard and sandwich them together again. If the mushrooms are large, cut them in half. Separate the halved onions into sections. Brush 4 skewers with oil and thread the sausage sandwiches and vegetables to balance well for colour and texture. Season with salt and pepper and brush with oil. Place under a hot grill for 12–15 minutes, turning the skewers occasionally.

Serves 4

Sausage Boats

Make the filling the night before and push it into a piping bag. Nothing to do in the morning but cook the sausages and squeeze the tube!

2 eggs, hard boiled and shelled
2 tablespoons tomato sauce
25 g (1 oz) fresh white breadcrumbs
1 teaspoon mustard powder

25 g (1 oz) butter, softened
salt and freshly-ground black pepper
8 large sausages

Mash the eggs thoroughly in a bowl. Beat the tomato sauce, breadcrumbs, mustard and butter into the eggs and season well. Put the mixture into a piping bag with a large plain nozzle. Grill or fry the sausages and when they are cooked slit each one not quite in half, lengthwise. Pipe a thick line of the egg mixture into each sausage.

Serves 4

Sausage Foldovers

Sausages wrapped in potato scone mixture make a neat breakfast package.

900 g (2 lb) potatoes, boiled
100 g (4 oz) flour
100 g (4 oz) butter, softened
salt and black pepper

8 sausages, grilled
mustard
1 egg, beaten

Put the potatoes into a large bowl and mash them thoroughly. Work in the flour and beat in the butter. Season well with salt and pepper. On a lightly-floured board, knead the mixture into a soft dough, shape into a roll and cut into 8 equal portions. Roll or pat each portion into a square. Place a cooked sausage in the centre of each and spread generously with mustard. Fold over the dough, press the edges together and pinch into flutes. Place the foldovers on a greased baking tray and brush with the beaten egg. You can prepare the meal to this stage the night before and then, in the morning, bake at 200°C (400°F)/Gas 6 for 30 minutes, until well risen and golden brown.

Serves 4

Friar's Omelette *(photograph facing page 36)*

Garlic croûtons add a pungent crunchiness to this tomato omelette.

3 thick slices white bread, without
  crusts
50 g (2 oz) butter
1 large clove garlic, peeled and
  crushed
2 tomatoes, skinned and chopped

8 eggs
salt and freshly-ground black
  pepper
½ teaspoon mixed dried herbs
6 black olives, stoned and sliced
  (optional)

Cut the bread into small cubes. Heat the butter in a large omelette pan or electric cook pan, add the garlic and bread cubes and fry, stirring occasionally, until golden brown. Add the tomatoes. Beat the eggs with the salt, pepper and herbs and pour into the pan (add a little more butter if necessary). Shake the pan until the mixture begins to set. Fold the omelette over to form a Swiss roll shape and tip on to a heated serving plate. Garnish with olive slices if liked.

Serves 4

Parmentier Eggs

Cook extra potatoes the day before, to have the main ingredient ready, and then it's a one-pot dish in the morning.

50 g (2 oz) butter	*salt and freshly-ground black pepper*
675 g (1½ lb) potatoes, boiled and	*8 eggs*
cubed	*150 ml (¼ pint) single cream*

Melt the butter in a fireproof dish and fry the potato cubes, stirring occasionally, until they are brown and crisp. Season well with salt and pepper and break the eggs on top. Add a little seasoning to the cream and pour it over the eggs. Bake at 200°C (400°F)/Gas 6 for 8–10 minutes. Serve with granary bread.

Serves 4

Morning Pizzas

Crumpets are not only for Sunday tea by the fire. Here they replace a scone base for a quick morning savoury. You can assemble the pizzas in advance and leave them all ready to grill.

8 crumpets	*100 g (4 oz) cheese, grated*
25 g (1 oz) butter	*2 rashers bacon, without rind*
2 teaspoons French mustard	*olives or capers for decoration*
5 tomatoes, thickly sliced	*(optional)*

Toast the underside of the crumpets until brown, then lightly toast the other side. Spread the second side with butter, then with mustard. Arrange the tomato slices, sprinkle with grated cheese then with thin strips of bacon. Decorate, if you like, with slices of olive or capers. Return to the grill and toast until the cheese melts.

Serves 4

Egg Pilaff

Beaten eggs stirred into steaming hot rice scramble on impact—it's an interesting combination.

750 ml (1¼ pints) chicken stock, hot	pinch of cayenne pepper
(see page 24)	225 g (8 oz) long-grain rice
salt and freshly-ground black	3 eggs, beaten
pepper	50 g (2 oz) cheese, grated

Season the stock well and cook the rice in it over a low heat until it is tender (about 35–40 minutes), adding a little more stock if necessary. Remove the pan from the heat and quickly stir in the beaten eggs. Turn the rice out on to a heated serving dish and sprinkle with the grated cheese.

Serves 4–6

Kedgeree

No breakfast chapter would be complete without kedgeree, the dish that is said to have featured on every self-respecting sideboard at breakfast time.

4 eggs, hard boiled	salt and cayenne pepper
175 g (6 oz) long-grain rice	1 egg, beaten
175 g (6 oz) smoked haddock fillet	1 tablespoon fresh chopped
50 g (2 oz) butter	parsley

Shell the eggs, slice one and chop the rest. Cook the rice in boiling salted water for 15 minutes and drain. Simmer the haddock for about 10 minutes, and drain. You can prepare the dish to this stage the night before.

Melt the butter in a saucepan, add the rice and flaked fish and stir with a fork until hot. Mix in the chopped eggs and season well. Stir in the beaten egg and serve hot, garnished with the sliced egg and parsley.

Serves 4

Mumbled Eggs

Even people who profess not to like 'cooked' breakfast at all couldn't resist this light turning of eggs in cream cheese.

8 eggs	50 g (2 oz) mushrooms, chopped
2 teaspoons made mustard	25 g (1 oz) butter
salt and freshly-ground black	50 g (2 oz) cream cheese
pepper	1 tablespoon cream

Beat the eggs with the mustard and season with salt and pepper. Stir in the mushrooms. Melt the butter in a pan over a low heat, add the egg mixture and stir until it begins to set. Stir in the cheese and cook for 2–3 minutes, still stirring. Fold in the cream and serve at once with triangles of crisp toast.

Serves 4

Humpties

Hard-boiling the eggs is the slowest part of this recipe, which presents bacon and eggs in a different way.

8 rashers streaky bacon, without rind
4 thin slices of white bread, buttered
8 eggs, hard boiled and shelled

Stretch the bacon with the back of a knife blade. Cut the bread slices in half lengthwise. Wrap each egg in bread (buttered side to the inside), then in bacon, and secure with a cocktail stick. Grill for 3 minutes on each side or put the humpties on a greased baking tray and bake near the top of the oven at 220°C (425°F)/Gas 7 for 5 minutes. Turn the rolls over and bake for a further 3 minutes, until crisp on both sides. Serve hot or cold with hot, buttered toast.

Serves 4

Bacon Loaf

The perfect 'brunch' dish, you can prepare this the night before and set it to cook in the oven with an automatic timer. Or cook it in advance and serve it cold.

550 g (1¼ lb) bacon slipper joint
1 medium-sized onion, peeled
100 g (4 oz) fresh white
  breadcrumbs
¼ teaspoon mixed dried herbs
freshly-ground black pepper

1 tablespoon fresh chopped parsley
¼ teaspoon grated lemon rind
1 egg, beaten
3 rashers streaky bacon, without
  rind

Bring the bacon joint to the boil, drain it and remove the rind and some of the fat. Dice the meat and mince it with the onion. Mix in the remaining ingredients, except the bacon rashers. Stretch the rashers and lay them in a greased 450-g (1-lb) loaf tin. Turn the bacon mixture into the tin and cover with foil. Stand the tin in a roasting pan containing a little water and cook at 170°C (325°F)/Gas 3 for 1½ hours. Serve hot or cold.

Serves 6

SOUPS

A soup is whatever you like to make it. It can be a pale and delicate opening to a formal meal, the dish that cleanses and excites the palate and gets the meal off to an encouraging start, or a whole meal in a pot, a lusty offering that calls for healthy appetites and hearty appreciation. Or, literally, any stage in between. But practically without exception, a soup can be only as good as the stock you use to make it. As you will see from the huge variety of recipes that follow, from one pot of basic stock you can concoct soups as varied as you like. Although the flavour of the stock will ultimately be masked by the individual ingredients, be they meat, fish, vegetables or fruit, the quality will always be there, the hidden secret of vital importance.

Above all things, stock benefits from long, slow, patient cooking and every cook will provide this by the cheapest and most convenient means at her disposal. For me, this means keeping a pot simmering on the solid-fuel cooker for several hours, while the broth extracts the very last morsel of flavour and goodness from the ingredients. Indeed, with the oven always alight, and the heat there for the using, it seems wasteful not to make several batches of different stocks every week.

But testing recipes for this chapter I have sometimes turned my back on this source of constant heat, and experimented with other appliances, far less costly to come by than my farmhouse cooker. So I have made numerous and delicious stocks and soups in a pressure cooker—an ideal way of cutting corners in time without sacrificing quality—and in electric slow cookers.

The basic stocks
The main basic stocks are **clear brown stock** (page 18), made with veal and beef, which is perfect for consommé, bortsch, jellied soups and others where clarity is an important part of the presentation; **brown bone stock** (page 22), which gives a good meaty flavour to minestrone and onion soups, among others; and **chicken stock** (page 24), which is the basis of soups as varied as artichoke or avocado, banana or beansprout. Basic **fish stock** (page 33), simply made with trimmings from the fishmonger's, makes all fish soups far more exciting, giving you a double chance to catch the flavour of the sea. **Vegetable stock** (page 31) has the same effect on vegetable soups,

strengthening the broth yet leaving the main ingredients to assert their characteristic flavour. In the recipes that follow, most of the vegetable soups are made from a base of chicken stock, because many people prefer the effect it has of giving the soup slightly more 'body'. However, vegetable stock can be substituted where chicken stock is recommended, and of course vegetarians would naturally do this. **White stock** (page 31), made with veal, can also be substituted for chicken stock and is used for light meat soups.

All the ingredients used for stocks should be the best you can afford and, needless to say, meat, bones and fish should be perfectly fresh. Most butchers will let you have a bag of bones or meat trimmings for soup at a relatively low cost. And as you delve into the housekeeping purse to pay for them, remember that a good, filling soup can actually take the place of a meat meal once or twice a week—but don't tell the butcher that! If he is an obliging sort, ask him to chop the bones into pieces as small as possible, for this is the way to extract the flavour and gelatine, which gives the stock a good set. This is essential for clear brown stock if you are to turn it into one of the jellied soups.

No stock should be vigorously boiled—it causes the albumen to solidify and results in scum; and no soup should be boiled after adding cream, yoghurt or egg yolks. When stock or soup is boiled, as in a pressure cooker, remove all trace of scum. It might be necessary, too, to adjust the seasoning.

Well-reduced stocks can be stored for several days in lidded polythene containers or screw-top jars (but *not* metal containers) in the refrigerator; in really hot weather it is advisable to bring the stock just to the boil every other day, cool it and store again. If the stock is *not* refrigerated, you must do this every day. The practice of keeping a stockpot on the stove day and night for weeks, adding bones and vegetables to it as they came to hand, is frowned upon now. In these bacteria-conscious times one cannot help wondering what creatures might find the warm conditions ideal for rapid growth and multiplication!

After simmering, all stocks should be carefully strained in a sieve through scalded muslin and left overnight to cool. Then you can easily lift off the layer of fat that will have risen to the top—far easier than trying to skim floating fat particles from the top of warm soup. I always seem to succeed in pushing them all to the bottom again!

Stocks keep in perfect condition in the freezer, so make them in large batches to draw on another time. Freeze some of your favourite soups, too— quantities in this chapter allow you to do so—but don't tie up all your capital, your basic stocks, in individual recipes. It won't leave you enough room to experiment with others.

Of course, if you have no reserve of any kind of stock and no time to make it, you can use a stock cube. But do not expect it to give you the depth of flavour and the satisfaction of a broth you have created.

The recipes in this chapter are set out in sections, giving first the instructions to make one of the basic stocks, then a collection of the recipes that arise from it; then another stock, and so on, to make the selection of recipes easier. If you have, say, chicken stock and want to turn it into an interesting soup, take your pick from the recipes that follow the basic one.

Serve your soup in shallow plates or small cups—a matter of preference, by the way, not etiquette. Jellied consommé, for example, is traditionally served in cups; but this is just because it is easier than chasing a cube of jelly round a large shallow bowl. Unless the soup is of the main-meal type, allow about 300 ml ($\frac{1}{2}$ pint) per person and, however simple the meal, always add a touch of garnish. No matter how delicious, soup cannot compete visually with, for instance, a pistachio pilaff or a melon filled with citrus fruit. And so garnishing is very important. Even a few croûtons and a sprinkling of chopped chives, a swirl of fresh or soured cream and a pinch of paprika, will prove variations in both texture and colour. There are suggestions for the appropriate garnishes with the recipes throughout the chapter, and a section at the end on how to prepare or make them.

Clear Brown Stock

The object is to achieve a stock which has a strong, meaty flavour, yet is as clear as a glass of water. To do this, you must remove every trace of scum that rises to the surface during simmering, and the solid layer of fat that settles on the top when it cools.

1·35 kg (3 lb) shin of beef, including bones	*1 large leek, washed and chopped*
1 large hambone	*2 stalks celery, washed and sliced*
450 g (1 lb) knuckle of veal	*1 bouquet garni*
2 large onions, peeled and chopped	*4·5 litres (8 pints) cold water*
2 large carrots, peeled and sliced	*a few peppercorns*
1 medium-sized turnip, peeled and roughly chopped (optional)	*1 tablespoon rock salt*

Roughly chop the meat, discarding any fat and gristle. If the butcher has not already done it for you, chop the bones as small as you can. This releases more gelatine and is important for a good stock. Put the meat and bones into a roasting pan with the onions, carrots and turnip if used and place in a hot oven, 220°C (425°F)/Gas 7, for about 25–30 minutes, until brown. Turn the meat and vegetables into a very large saucepan and add the leek, celery, herbs and water. The water *must* be cold; never start a stock with warm or hot water to try to hasten the process. Bring slowly to the boil and simmer gently for about 2 hours, skimming off any scum at intervals. Add the peppercorns and salt, and simmer for a further 3 hours, skimming occasionally.

Strain through a sieve lined with scalded muslin and leave overnight.

When the stock is cold, lift off the lid of fat. To use the stock, which should have set to a firm jelly, scrape away the sediment from the bottom. You can store this stock in a freezer, or in a refrigerator, in covered jars or boxes, for several days.

Makes about 4·5 litres (8 pints)

Consommé

To some cooks, there is as much an aura of mystery surrounding the making of consommé as there is to others about baking with yeast. Consommé is a development of clear brown stock, further enriched with beef and vegetables. It is clarified with egg whites and egg shells—a much simpler process than it sounds.

2·25 litres (4 pints) clear brown stock, cold
225 g (8 oz) shin of beef, minced
1 medium-sized onion, peeled and chopped
1 large carrot, peeled or scraped and chopped
1 stalk celery, washed and chopped
1 bayleaf, crushed
bunch of fresh herbs, tied together
few peppercorns
2 egg whites, whisked
2 egg shells, crushed
1 small glass medium sherry
salt
pinch of sugar
cheese straws or cheese scones, to serve (optional)

Put the stock, minced beef, prepared vegetables, herbs and peppercorns into a large saucepan. Add the whisked egg whites and the crushed shells. Using a wire whisk, whisk until the soup comes just to the boiling point, then simmer, without whisking, for a few minutes. Remove the pan from the heat and allow to settle. Strain through 2 thicknesses of scalded muslin (it is easiest to do this if you line a sieve with muslin). Return the soup to the pan, add the sherry, salt and a pinch of sugar and bring slowly to the boil again.

Serve at once, with cheese straws or cheese scones, or chill in the refrigerator and serve when it is lightly jellied.

Serves 8

There are a number of classic French ways of serving consommé, the individual names varying according to the garnish used. *Consommé Brunoise* has a garnish of diced, cooked vegetables such as carrots and turnips; *Consommé Dustan* is served with cooked dried haricot beans (you could turn a few left-over beans to advantage for this); and *Consommé Impératrice* has a lightly-poached egg added to each portion—practically a meal in itself.

Jellied consommé can be cut into cubes, like those in a coloured packet jelly, and served sprinkled with fresh chopped parsley and a wedge of lemon.

It is also a very good filling for avocado pears, to serve as a first course, or, mixed with ice-cold melon balls, as a salad to accompany, say, cold roast pork.

Jellied Madrilène *(photograph facing page 37)*

The addition of tomato purée makes this version of cold consommé very rich fare. Serve the jellied soup chopped into cubes or, for a salad, set in a mould and garnished with thin slices of fresh tomato.

1·2 litres (2 pints) clear brown stock
450 ml (¾ pint) tomato purée

25 g (1 oz) gelatine (2 envelopes)
watercress and fresh tomatoes to garnish

Put the stock in a pan with the tomato purée and bring slowly to boiling point. Meanwhile, sprinkle the gelatine on to a little cold water in a cup, stand in a pan of hot water and stir until dissolved. Stir it into the hot soup until thoroughly blended. Strain the soup into flat ice-cube trays and leave until cold, then cut into small cubes. If serving as a salad, pour instead into a wetted mould and leave until set. Garnish with watercress and thinly sliced tomatoes.

Serves 4–6

Bortsch

To live up to its reputation as one of the finest of Russian dishes, a good bortsch is not just a beef stock with beetroot, though those are the principle ingredients. It is strengthened by a crop of other vegetables, and enriched with butter and soured cream.

2·25 litres (4 pints) clear brown stock
1 hambone, weighing about 450 g (1 lb)
1 tablespoon red wine vinegar
450 g (1 lb) beetroot, raw
25 g (1 oz) butter
450 g (1 lb) cabbage, cored and shredded
2 large onions, peeled and chopped
2 large carrots, peeled or scraped and chopped

1 large parsnip, peeled and grated
225 g (8 oz) potatoes, peeled and diced
1 small can tomato purée
salt and freshly-ground black pepper
pinch of sugar
2 tablespoons fresh chopped parsley
150-g (5-oz) carton fresh soured cream to garnish

Pour the stock into a large flameproof casserole, add the hambone and vinegar and bring slowly to the boil. Wash, peel and grate the beetroot, add to the stock and bring again to boiling point. Take the casserole off the heat and leave to 'sweat' for about 20 minutes, while the hot stock draws the colour from the beetroot.

Heat the butter in a frying pan and add the prepared vegetables. Sauté gently for 4–5 minutes, add the tomato purée and season with salt, pepper and a pinch of sugar. Stir well to blend, then turn the vegetable mixture into the stock in the casserole. Bring gradually to the boil and simmer gently for 45 minutes. Trim the meat from the bone, cut in chunks and return to the casserole, discarding the bone. Stir in the parsley and serve the soup hot with a spoonful of soured cream topping each portion.

Serves 8–10

Rice and Aubergine Soup

In some Mediterranean countries where aubergines are cheap and plentiful, they make this soup with a higher proportion of vegetables, and with water. You will find that the soup is deeper, more interesting, if you draw from your supply of clear brown stock.

5 tablespoons olive oil	*225 g (8 oz) tomatoes, skinned and*
450 g (1 lb) aubergines, peeled and	*chopped*
diced	*2·25 litres (4 pints) clear brown*
2 large onions, peeled and finely	*stock*
chopped	*50 g (2 oz) long-grain rice*
2 large cloves garlic, peeled and	*salt and freshly-ground black*
crushed	*pepper*
½ teaspoon dried basil	*croûtons to garnish (see page 37)*

Heat the oil in a flameproof casserole, add the diced aubergines and fry over a medium heat until the vegetable begins to turn brown. Add the onion, garlic, dried herb and tomato. Stir well and cook until the onion is soft but not brown. Add the stock, bring slowly to the boil and simmer for 20 minutes. Add the rice, bring back to boiling point and simmer for another 15 minutes. Taste and season with salt and pepper. Garnish with croûtons.

Serves 8

Mulligatawny

There have over the years been cheap and nasty imposters of this soup, inferior brews with a teaspoon of curry powder stirred in. But with good clear stock you can produce a masterpiece.

½ teaspoon cardamom seeds
½ teaspoon cumin seeds
½ teaspoon mustard seeds
few black peppercorns
2–3 juniper berries
2 bayleaves, crushed
thinly-pared rind of ½ small lemon
50 g (2 oz) butter

2 large onions, peeled and finely
 chopped
1 heaped teaspoon curry powder
50 g (2 oz) flour
2·25 litres (4 pints) clear brown
 stock
salt
grated rind of 1 large orange to
 garnish

Crush the spices in a pestle and mortar, or in a bowl with the back of a strong tablespoon. Tie them in muslin with the crushed bayleaves and lemon peel. Melt the butter in a large flameproof casserole, add the onion and sauté gently until it is just beginning to brown. Add the curry powder and flour, stir well and cook for 3 minutes. Gradually add the stock, a ladleful at a time, and stir well to blend. Add the bag of spices and simmer for 20 minutes, when the soup will have thickened, then continue simmering very gently for 10 minutes. Taste and season with salt. Remove the bag of spices. Sprinkle with grated orange rind before serving piping hot.

Serves 8

Brown Bone Stock

Without the shin of beef used in the making of clear brown stock, this stock has a slightly less pronounced meat flavour. Any combinations of vegetables can be added to give it character.

25 g (1 oz) butter
900 g (2 lb) beef bones, chopped
 small
1 knuckle of veal
50 g (2 oz) fat bacon with rinds,
 roughly chopped
2 large onions, peeled and chopped

2 large carrots, peeled or scraped
 and sliced
1 bouquet garni
few black peppercorns
rock salt
2·25 litres (4 pints) cold water

Melt the butter in a heavy casserole or saucepan. Trim the meat from the bones. Put the bones, meat, bacon and prepared vegetables into the casserole and brown in a hot oven or over a high heat. Add the herbs and seasoning, pour in the water and bring to the boil, skimming the surface occasionally to remove the scum as it rises. Cover and simmer gently for 4½–5 hours, skimming from time to time. Remove stock from heat, allow to settle, then strain through 2 layers of scalded muslin lining a sieve. When the stock is cold lift the lid of fat from the top. Leave any sediment in the bowl when using the stock.

You can keep the bones and vegetables in the refrigerator and add more to them to make a second batch of stock which, though less tasty than the first, would be adequate for gravy, sauces and meat casserole dishes.

Makes about 2·25 litres (4 pints)

Minestrone

To make this soup look as attractive as the Italians do, it is worth taking the trouble to cut the vegetables into even-sized pieces. A mandoline cutter is a great help in making paper-thin carrot 'pennies'. It is easier to cut the celery and bacon with sharp kitchen scissors than to chop them with a knife.

1·8 litres (3 pints) brown bone stock
2 stalks celery, with leaves, washed and finely cut
2 large carrots, peeled or scraped and finely sliced into 'pennies'
100 g (4 oz) bacon, without rind, finely chopped
100 g (4 oz) pasta shapes

1 large onion, peeled and thinly sliced
225 g (8 oz) tomatoes, skinned and sliced
salt and freshly-ground black pepper
175 g (6 oz) Parmesan cheese, freshly grated, to garnish

Put the stock in a large flameproof casserole and bring slowly to the boil. Add the celery, carrots and bacon, bring back to boiling point and simmer for about 30 minutes. Add the onion, tomato and pasta and season with salt and pepper. Bring to the boil again and simmer for 25 minutes. Serve piping hot, thickly sprinkled with the grated Parmesan cheese.

Serves 6

Lentil Soup *(photograph facing page 37)*

Almost a meal in itself, this rich, red soup could be served with green salad and hot, crusty bread for a light but filling lunch.

50 g (2 oz) butter
1 medium-sized onion, peeled and sliced
2 stalks celery, washed and chopped
25 g (1 oz) flour
1·2 litres (2 pints) brown bone stock
225 g (8 oz) brown lentils, soaked

3 large tomatoes, skinned and sliced
1 teaspoon lemon juice, strained
salt and freshly-ground black pepper
croûtons to garnish (see page 37)
small cubes of Cheddar cheese or thin slices of frankfurter sausage to garnish (optional)

Melt the butter in a large saucepan, add the onion and celery and sauté for 4–5 minutes over a low heat. Stir in the flour to form a roux, then add the stock a little at a time, stirring until the liquor thickens a little. Add the lentils and tomatoes, cover and bring gradually to the boil. Skim the surface, then simmer for 1 hour. Put the mixture in an electric blender or rub through a sieve, and pour back into the pan. Add the lemon juice and season well. Serve hot, garnished with croûtons and, to make the dish more substantial, tiny cubes of Cheddar cheese or thin slices of frankfurter sausage.

Serves 4

French Onion Soup

There are many ways of making French onion soup, and in its country of origin the recipe varies from one region or even one village to another. If you use good-quality brown bone stock, French bread and Gruyère cheese (not sliced bread and Cheddar) you will have created a satisfying dish.

50 g (2 oz) butter
675 g (1½ lb) onions, peeled and
* thinly sliced*
2·25 litres (4 pints) brown bone
* stock*
salt and freshly-ground black pepper

16 slices dry French bread, cut
* slantwise on loaf*
225 g (8 oz) Gruyère cheese,
* freshly grated*

Melt the butter in a heavy saucepan. Add the onions and cook, stirring, until brown. This gives the soup its characteristic 'dark' flavour. Gradually add the stock, stirring well to blend with the onions, then bring slowly to the boil. Season with salt and pepper. To serve, pour the soup into deep bowls, float 2 slices of bread on each one and sprinkle liberally with grated cheese. Flash under a hot grill to brown the top.

Serves 8

Chicken Stock

This is the most versatile stock of all, providing as it does a lightly-flavoured and pale-coloured background to an infinite variety of vegetable and fruit additions. I would go so far as to say that no cook should ever discard a chicken carcass without first making stock; it really is throwing money and culinary enjoyment down the drain. A cooked chicken carcass can be used to make stock, but it will be darker and the flavour less subtle. To produce a really delicate stock, use a whole raw boiling fowl. Once the stock is made, you can remove the meat from the carcass and use some of the stock for a sauce.

25 g (1 oz) butter
1 raw chicken carcass, 1·2–1·35 kg
  (2½–3 lb), chopped small
chicken giblets and claws,
  thoroughly washed
1 pork bone, chopped small (if
  available)
2 large onions, peeled and sliced

2 large carrots, peeled or scraped
  and sliced
1 stalk celery, washed and chopped
1 piece fresh green ginger, scraped
  and sliced
2·25 litres (4 pints) water
1 bouquet garni
salt

Melt the butter in a large saucepan and add the chicken carcass, giblets and claws, the pork bone if used and the prepared vegetables. Cook over a fairly high heat until beginning to brown. Add the water, herbs and salt, bring slowly to the boil and simmer for about 3½–4 hours, skimming occasionally. Remove from the heat, allow to settle for a few minutes, then strain into a bowl through 2 thicknesses of scalded muslin lining a sieve. Leave to cool, then remove the fat that has settled on top.

Makes about 2·25 litres (4 pints)

Cream of Avocado Soup

This is a chilled soup, to serve in the summer under the sunlight or the stars. Ideally, as with all chilled soups, it should be served in a bowl standing in a dish of crushed ice. But if this is not practicable, thoroughly chill the tureen and the serving bowls and garnish with small sprigs of cool-looking fresh mint.

2 very ripe avocado pears
juice and grated rind of 1 small
  lemon
1·2 litres (2 pints) chicken stock
300 ml (½ pint) double cream
pinch of cayenne pepper
salt and freshly-ground white
  pepper

75 ml (⅛ pint) whipping cream
extra, thin slices of avocado pear,
  dipped in lemon juice (optional)
sprigs of fresh mint to garnish
  (optional)

Cut the avocado pears in half, remove the stones and scoop the flesh from the skins. Mash it in a bowl with the strained lemon juice, which will prevent the flesh from discolouring and give a slight tang to the soup. Stir in the lemon rind. Rub the pulp through a nylon sieve (not a metal one) and put in a flameproof pan. Over a low heat, gradually stir in the chicken stock, blending well and bring slowly to the boil, stirring occasionally. Take care that the mixture does not 'catch' at the bottom. Add the cream, a pinch of cayenne pepper, salt and white pepper and stir well. Allow to cool and then put in the refrigerator or a very cold place to chill. Serve in chilled bowls, garnished with swirls of lightly-whipped cream and topped by small sprigs of fresh mint or thin slices of fresh avocado pear dipped in lemon juice.

Serves 6

Cream of Artichoke Soup

Anyone who grows artichokes will probably know and love this soup, or a version of it. Anyone who doesn't will be delighted by it—and will surely ask what it is.

900 g (2 lb) Jerusalem artichokes,
 thoroughly scrubbed and scraped
juice of 1 lemon, strained
50 g (2 oz) butter
2 large onions, peeled and sliced
rind of ½ orange, thinly pared
1·5 litres (2½ pints) chicken stock

300 ml (½ pint) single cream
salt and freshly-ground black pepper
75 ml (⅛ pint) whipping cream, to
 garnish
rind of remaining ½ orange, grated,
 or very thin slices of orange, to
 garnish

As you scrape or peel the artichokes, put them at once into a bowl of cold water with the lemon juice, to prevent them from discolouring. Melt the butter in a large saucepan, add the onions and pared orange rind and sauté for 4–5 minutes over a low heat, stirring once or twice. Remove the artichokes from the water with a straining spoon, pat them dry on kitchen paper and slice them. Turn them over in the butter as quickly as possible to coat them thoroughly. Sauté all the vegetables gently for about 5 minutes, stirring occasionally. Add the chicken stock, bring to the boil and skim the surface. Simmer for 20–25 minutes. Remove the orange rind. Put the mixture in an electric blender, a little at a time, or press through a sieve. Stir in the single cream and season with salt and pepper. To serve, return the soup to the pan and reheat without boiling, garnish with swirls of lightly-whipped cream and a scattering of grated orange rind or with thin slices of fresh orange topped with the cream.

Serves 6

Banana Soup

It seems a far cry from chicken stock to bananas, but this recipe bridges the gap with a strongly-flavoured, creamy soup that would be a talking point at a dinner party—and it's quick to make, too. This soup does not freeze satisfactorily.

26

6 bananas, peeled and mashed
1·5 litres (2½ pints) chicken stock
salt
pinch of ground mace

grated rind of 1 large orange
1 teaspoon arrowroot (optional)
3 slices rich malt fruit loaf to
garnish

Rub the bananas through a nylon (not metal) sieve and gradually stir in the chicken stock. Season with a little salt and a pinch of mace and stir in the grated orange rind. Pour the mixture into a large flameproof casserole and bring slowly to the boil. If you prefer a thicker soup, mix 1 teaspoon of arrowroot with a little cold water and stir into the soup. Bring to boiling point and simmer, stirring, for 3 minutes. Serve the soup hot. To garnish, remove the crust from the malt loaf, cut into cubes and float on top.

Serves 6

Broccoli Cream Soup

Rather like cauliflower soup, but with a stronger, 'greener' flavour, this recipe can be a welcome way to use a garden glut or a special treat with fresh or frozen broccoli.

25 g (1 oz) butter
1 medium-sized onion, peeled and
sliced
1 stalk celery, washed and finely
chopped
1 large potato, peeled and sliced

550 g (1¼ lb) broccoli, washed and
broken into 5-cm (2-in) lengths
1·2 litres (2 pints) chicken stock
150 ml (¼ pint) single cream
salt and freshly-ground black pepper
croûtons to garnish (see page 37)

Melt the butter in a large saucepan. Add the onion and celery and fry gently for 4–5 minutes without browning. Add the potato and broccoli, pour in the stock and stir well. Bring slowly to the boil, then simmer gently for 20–25 minutes, until the vegetables are tender. Remove from heat, allow to cool a little, then purée in a blender or rub through a sieve. Return to the rinsed pan, stir in the cream and season with salt and pepper. Reheat but do not boil. Serve garnished with croûtons.

Serves 6

Chicken, Egg and Lemon Soup *(Avgalemono)*

For a change, a chicken-stock soup that actually tastes of chicken! This one is a traditional dish of Greece, where the cooling tang of the lemon is welcome on a hot day.

1·2 litres (2 pints) chicken stock
100 g (4 oz) long-grain rice
salt and freshly-ground black pepper
3 eggs, separated

1 teaspoon water
juice of 2 lemons, strained
thin slices of lemon to garnish

Pour the chicken stock into a large flameproof casserole and bring slowly to the boil. Skim if necessary. Add the rice, stir well, and bring to the boil again. Cover and simmer for 12–15 minutes, then remove from heat. Season with salt and pepper. Whisk the egg whites with 1 teaspoon of water, then add the yolks and continue whisking until pale and fluffy. Add the strained lemon juice and then, gradually, a little of the warm stock. Pour the egg mixture into the casserole, whisk to blend thoroughly, and reheat but do not allow to boil. Garnish with a twist of lemon.

Serves 4

Cock-a-leekie

One of Britain's best-known meals-in-a-pot, cock-a-leekie soup is a bland but tasty combination of chicken, vegetables and broth.

1 1·35-kg (3-lb) boiling fowl
2·8 litres (5 pints) water
8 large leeks, washed and cut into
  5-cm (2-in) lengths

75 g (3 oz) pearl barley
salt
2 tablespoons fresh chopped parsley,
  to garnish

Thoroughly wash the bird and trim off the large areas of fat. Wrap in a piece of muslin and put in a very large saucepan or flameproof casserole, cover with the water and bring rapidly to the boil. Skim the surface, then add the leeks, pearl barley and salt. Bring to the boil again and simmer, skimming occasionally, for 2½–3 hours, when the meat will be coming away from the bones. Remove the bird, allow to cool a little, then take off the skin. Take the meat from the bones and cut it into small chunks. Return the meat to the broth and reheat. Taste and add more salt if needed. Serve the meat, leeks and broth in deep soup plates, well sprinkled with parsley, and provide plenty of hot, crusty bread.

Serves 6–8

Corn Chowder

I'm all for adapting and experimenting with recipes, but whatever you do don't leave out the bacon in this one. Somehow that's what gives the sweetcorn its flavour.

100 g (4 oz) streaky bacon, without rind, diced
1 large onion, peeled and chopped
25 g (1 oz) flour
450 ml (¾ pint) milk
450 ml (¾ pint) chicken stock
350 g (¾ lb) sweetcorn kernels

450 g (1 lb) potatoes, peeled, parboiled and diced
300 ml (½ pint) single cream
freshly-ground black pepper
cayenne pepper to garnish
fresh chopped chives to garnish

Put the diced bacon into a large flameproof casserole over a fairly high heat, so that the fat runs. Add the onion and cook until it is just turning pale golden. Add the flour, stir well, then gradually add the milk, stirring. When the mixture begins to thicken, gradually pour in the chicken stock, still stirring. (The milk and stock will blend in better if they are warm.) Add the sweetcorn and the diced potato and slowly bring to the boil. Simmer for 10–12 minutes, stirring occasionally, then pour in the cream, blend well and season with pepper. Reheat without boiling. Garnish with a pinch of cayenne pepper and chopped chives.

Serves 4

Beansprout Soup

Some supermarkets and health food shops sell fresh beansprouts now, and they are remarkably cheap. And it's easy to grow your own, mustard-and-cress fashion, on damp flannel or in a jam jar. They make an interesting, crunchy addition to a light chicken stock.

1·2 litres (2 pints) chicken stock
225 g (8 oz) fresh beansprouts, washed
100 g (4 oz) pasta shapes, cooked
175 g (6 oz) cooked chicken, shredded

½ teaspoon soy sauce
salt and freshly-ground black pepper
celery leaves, finely chopped, to garnish

Put the stock into a large flameproof casserole and bring to the boil. Add the beansprouts, return to the boil and simmer for 3 minutes. Add the pasta and chicken and simmer until they are heated through. Season with soy sauce, salt and pepper and serve with a sprinkling of finely-chopped celery leaves.

Serves 4

Chick Pea Soup

Mediterranean cooks use mint in cooking much more than we do in Britain. Here it is indistinguishable but important in a thick, winter soup.

225 g (8 oz) dried chick peas,
  soaked overnight (see page 42)
3 large cloves garlic, peeled and
  crushed
½ teaspoon salt

3 tablespoons fresh chopped mint
3 tablespoons fresh chopped parsley
3 tablespoons good olive oil
1·2 litres (2 pints) chicken stock
croûtons to garnish (see page 37)

Cook the chick peas in water, without salt, for 2½ hours until tender (or cook extra when you are serving them in another way), then drain. In a small bowl, or with a pestle and mortar, mix together the crushed garlic, salt, chopped herbs and olive oil to form a thick paste, with the consistency of mayonnaise. In a large flameproof casserole, bring the chicken stock slowly to the boil, skim the surface, then add the cooked chick peas. Bring to boiling point again, add the herb and oil paste and stir well. Serve with croûtons.

Serves 4–6

Watercress Soup

If I had to declare my hand, I would be bound to say that this is my all-time favourite soup, and it has been for years. In fact, I have to be stern with myself to avoid serving it with monotonous regularity to guests at dinner!

50 g (2 oz) butter
8 spring onions, washed, trimmed
  and finely chopped
3 bundles watercress, washed and
  chopped
25 g (1 oz) flour

1·8 litres (3 pints) chicken stock
salt and freshly-ground black pepper
2 egg yolks
150 ml (¼ pint) single cream
extra cream to garnish

Melt the butter in a large saucepan or flameproof casserole, add the spring onions and sauté over a low heat until they soften. Add the chopped watercress, reserving a few sprigs for a garnish, and stir well. Cook for another 5 minutes until the watercress collapses. Stir in the flour, cook for about 2 minutes, then gradually add the stock, stirring. Season with salt and pepper and bring to the boil. Simmer for 5–6 minutes, remove from the heat and allow to cool a little. Put the mixture in an electric blender, or rub through a sieve, and return to the pan. Heat to just below boiling point. Beat the egg yolks thoroughly, and beat in the cream. Add a little warm (not hot) soup to this mixture, then pour it into the pan and reheat without boiling. Garnish with a little extra cream and the reserved watercress.

Serves 6

White Stock

Made with knuckle of veal, this lightly-flavoured stock is interchangeable with chicken stock for most meat and vegetable soups. It is less often made now because we seem to have more chicken carcasses than knuckles of veal.

1·35-kg (3-lb) knuckle of veal, chopped small	1 bouquet garni
2 large onions, peeled and chopped	2·8 litres (5 pints) water
2 stalks celery, washed and chopped	salt and freshly-ground black pepper

Trim the meat from the bones, discarding any fat. Put the meat and the bones into a large saucepan with the prepared vegetables and herbs, and pour on the water. Season with salt and pepper, cover and bring slowly to the boil. Skim the surface, lower the heat and simmer for 4½–5 hours, skimming occasionally. Allow to cool a little, then strain into a bowl through a sieve lined with 2 layers of scalded muslin. When the stock is cold, lift off the lid of fat. Store in covered containers in the refrigerator or freezer.

Makes about 2·8 litres (5 pints)

Cheese Soup

Not when a large and varied selection of cheeses is a feature of your menu, or when you are offering cheesecake, but at any other time this unusual soup will be a winner.

25 g (1 oz) butter	salt and freshly-ground black pepper
50 g (2 oz) flour	2 egg yolks
100 g (4 oz) Gruyère cheese, grated	150 ml (¼ pint) single cream
1·2 litres (2 pints) white stock	croûtons to garnish (see page 37)

Melt the butter in a large flameproof casserole, stir in the flour and cook until it forms a roux. Add the grated cheese, remove from the heat, and stir well. Return the pan to the heat and gradually stir in the stock—it will blend better if you can heat it first. Season well. Cook until smooth and creamy, still stirring. Beat the egg yolks in a small bowl, beat in the cream and stir in a little of the warm soup. Pour the egg mixture into the casserole, heat without boiling and serve with plenty of crisp croûtons.

Serves 4

Vegetable Stock

Most vegetable and herb soups can be built up from a good vegetable stock. You can vary the actual vegetables you use, according to the season.

25 g (1 oz) butter
2 large onions, peeled and chopped
225 g (8 oz) carrots, peeled or
  scraped and chopped
225 g (8 oz) turnips, peeled and
  chopped
4 stalks celery, washed and chopped

225 g (8 oz) leeks, washed and
  chopped
3·3 litres (6 pints) water
1 bouquet garni
salt
few peppercorns

Melt the butter in a very large saucepan, add the vegetables and sauté over a low heat until they are soft but not brown. Pour in the water, add the herbs and season well. Bring to the boil and skim off any scum that rises. Simmer over a low heat for 3–3½ hours. Allow to cool a little, then strain into a bowl through a sieve lined with 2 layers of scalded muslin. When the stock has cooled, lift off the lid of fat. Store in lidded containers in the refrigerator or freezer.

Makes about 3·3 litres (6 pints)

Dill Soup

If it's a Russian recipe, the chances are that soured cream features somewhere in the contents list, and this soup is no exception. It is a good example of a herb soup based on vegetable stock.

25 g (1 oz) butter
1 bunch fresh dill, finely chopped
40 g (1½ oz) flour
1·2 litres (2 pints) vegetable stock
2 egg yolks
300 ml (½ pint) fresh soured cream

salt and freshly-ground black pepper
few dill seeds, crushed, to garnish
  (optional)
yolk of 1 hard-boiled egg, chopped,
  to garnish (optional)

Melt the butter in a large flameproof casserole, add the dill and cook over a low heat, stirring, for 3–4 minutes. Add the flour, stir until a roux forms, then gradually add the stock, stirring. (It will blend better if you heat it first.) Beat the egg yolks and, reserving a little to garnish, beat in the soured cream. Stir in a little of the warm stock, then pour the egg mixture into the casserole. Season well with salt and pepper. Heat to just below boiling point. Serve hot, each portion garnished with a blob of soured cream and a sprinkling of crushed dill seeds or the chopped hard-boiled egg yolk.

Serves 4

Julienne Soup

A soup in which the garnish—matchstick-thin strips of crisp, colourful vegetables—is an integral part of the recipe.

50 g (2 oz) butter	*2 leeks, washed and finely sliced*
1 large onion, peeled and thinly sliced	*2 cabbage leaves, core removed, shredded*
2 carrots, peeled or scraped and very thinly sliced	*1·2 litres (2 pints) vegetable stock*
2 small white turnips, peeled and very thinly sliced	*salt and freshly-ground black pepper*
	cheese straws to serve (see page 37)

Melt the butter in a large flameproof casserole, add the onion and sauté over a low heat until transparent. Add the remaining prepared vegetables and stir until they are all turned in the butter. Add the stock and bring to the boil. Skim the surface, then season well. Simmer for 12–15 minutes until the vegetables are just tender. Do not overcook them or the texture will be lost. If liked, serve with cheese straws.

Serves 4

Fish Stock

Even though Britain is an island, we do not have the variety and selection of fish that many other countries enjoy, so we cannot really compete on equal terms with some of the classic Continental fish soups. However, starting with a fish stock and adding further seafood to it, we can produce soups which do credit to our native love of the sea. Ask your fishmonger for fish heads, tails and trimmings—he will be glad you are taking an interest in his trade!

1·35 kg (3 lb) fish trimmings and bones, washed	*1 bayleaf*
2 large onions, peeled and chopped	*salt and freshly-ground black pepper*
1 stalk celery, washed and chopped	*juice of ½ small lemon, strained*
1 bunch fresh herbs	*1·8 litres (3 pints) water*
	150 ml (¼ pint) dry white wine or dry cider

Put all the ingredients together in a large saucepan, cover and bring slowly to the boil. Skim the surface of any scum that rises, lower the heat and simmer for 1 hour. Allow to cool slightly, then strain into a bowl through a sieve lined with 2 layers of scalded muslin. Store in lidded containers in a refrigerator for no more than 2–3 days, or in a freezer.

Makes scant 2 litres (3¼ pints)

Fish Soup with Spinach

The fish stock is used to poach both fillets of fish and spinach leaves. If you wish, you can increase the proportion of fish and serve the soup as a fish stew.

900 ml (1½ pints) fish stock
2 tablespoons olive oil
2 large potatoes, peeled and diced
1 bunch parsley
1 bayleaf
225 g (8 oz) white fish fillets,
  washed and skinned (such as cod,
  fresh haddock, coley)

3 large tomatoes, skinned and
  quartered
about 16 large leaves spinach,
  washed
salt and freshly-ground black pepper
juice of ½ lemon, strained
cayenne pepper to garnish

Put the fish stock in a large flameproof casserole with the olive oil, potatoes, parsley and bayleaf and bring slowly to the boil. Skim the surface, then simmer for 10 minutes. Add the fish fillets, tomatoes and spinach leaves and season well. Return just to boiling-point and simmer for a further 10 minutes. Remove parsley and bayleaf, add more seasoning if needed and stir in the lemon juice. Sprinkle sparingly with cayenne pepper before serving.

Serves 4

Fish Soup with Tomato

This is a cream of fish soup, like a rich, smooth sauce. Indeed, if you have any left over you can serve it as a sauce with grilled white fish or reduce it a little over a high heat and use it as a filling for savoury pancakes.

675 g (1½ lb) fillets of white fish,
  washed and skinned
1 large onion, peeled and sliced
1 stalk celery, washed and sliced
2 sprigs parsley
1 bayleaf
1·8 litres (3 pints) fish stock

1 small can tomato purée
150 ml (¼ pint) dry white wine or
  dry cider
salt and freshly-ground black pepper
croûtons (see page 37) and thin
  slices of lemon to garnish

Check that all the bones have been removed from the fish. Put it in a large saucepan or flameproof casserole with the onion, celery, parsley and bayleaf, pour on the stock and bring slowly to the boil. Skim the surface and simmer for 12–15 minutes. With a draining spoon, remove the parsley and bayleaf and put the fish, vegetables and stock in an electric blender, then sieve to make certain no bones or celery 'strings' remain. If you do not have a blender, rub the mixture through a sieve. Return the purée to the pan or casserole, stir in the tomato purée and wine or cider, and season well with salt and pepper. Serve garnished with croûtons and a twist of lemon.

Serves 6–8

Cucumber Fish Soup

The soft unmistakable texture of poached cucumber is a delightful surprise in this colourful soup which originated in Russia.

50 g (2 oz) butter
2 large onions, peeled and thinly
  sliced
1 red pepper, trimmed and thinly
  sliced
1 medium-sized cucumber, peeled,
  seeds removed and diced
1·2 litres (2 pints) fish stock

2 large tomatoes, skinned, seeds
  removed and chopped
450 g (1 lb) white fish fillets,
  washed and skinned
salt and freshly-ground black pepper
1 lemon, thinly sliced
1 tablespoon fresh chopped parsley

Melt the butter in a large flameproof casserole, add the onions and cook over a low heat until transparent. Add the red pepper and cucumber and cook for a further 2–3 minutes, without allowing to brown. Pour on the fish stock, add the tomatoes and the fish fillets and season well. Bring to the boil, skim the surface and simmer for 8–10 minutes, until the fish is tender but not breaking. With a draining spoon, remove the fish and flake into large pieces. Return to the casserole, add the lemon slices and check the seasoning. Reheat. Sprinkle with parsley to serve.

Serves 4–6

Prawn Chowder

Again, the bacon is the 'secret' ingredient, which stops the soup tasting too fishy yet heightens its interest.

50 g (2 oz) butter
50 g (2 oz) bacon, rind removed,
  diced
1 medium-sized onion, peeled and
  chopped
1 small green pepper, trimmed and
  thinly sliced
2 stalks celery, washed and finely
  chopped
900 ml (1½ pints) fish stock
1 bunch herbs

1 bayleaf
3 large tomatoes, skinned and
  quartered
225 g (8 oz) frozen prawns, peeled
salt and freshly-ground black pepper
cayenne pepper
little single cream to garnish
few unpeeled fresh prawns, if
  available, to garnish

Melt the butter in a flameproof casserole and add the bacon, onion, green pepper and celery. Cook over a low heat for 3–4 minutes, then pour on the fish stock. Add the herbs and bayleaf, bring slowly to the boil and skim the surface. Simmer for about 15 minutes. Add the tomatoes and prawns and season well. Return to the boil and simmer for a further 10 minutes. Remove the herbs and bayleaf. Serve with a swirl of cream on each portion. Garnish with 1 or 2 fresh unpeeled prawns per portion.

Serves 4

Garnishes

Most soups benefit in both taste and eye appeal from a last-minute garnish, however simple. To a large extent, the complexity of the garnish will be matched to the formality of the occasion. If friends have dropped in unexpectedly, and you are whipping up a soup from one of your basic stocks, you will not stop to make cheese straws or cheese scones to hand round with it. But if, on the other hand, the same soup is to open a meal guests have been looking forward to for some time, then these special offerings would play their part in making the whole meal memorable.

Many soups are garnished from within; minestrone, for example, is vibrant with its mixture of vegetables and pasta, all different colours and shapes, and needs no more than a sprinkling of grated cheese—and not necessarily even that. Julienne soup, too, is bright with vegetables, cooked to a crispness and cut matchstick-thin to look attractive.

Cream soups often give little clue to their identity, and here you can play the garnishing in either of two ways. You can decorate the soup with a little of the main ingredient—slices of fresh avocado pear, sprigs of fresh watercress or a pinch of dill seed—and give the game away from the beginning. Or you can keep your guests guessing until they take the first spoonful, and garnish a cream of artichoke soup with grated orange rind or the thinnest slices of orange—delicious with all root vegetable soups, actually—and banana soup with perky little cubes of rich malt loaf.

Croûtons, for all that they are fried in butter, are the traditional accompaniment to many of the richer soups, delicious with aubergine, cheese, and fish and tomato soups, among many others. Crisply fried to drying point, croûtons keep well in a covered container; it is useful to have a few always in reserve.

Then there are the garnishes that positively add substance to a soup. Cubes of strong cheese or slices of frankfurter sausages, for instance, turn lentil soup into an even heartier dish; slices of French bread thickly piled with grated Gruyère cheese cause French onion soup to take the edge off the keenest appetites, and small dumplings, maybe flavoured with caraway or dried herbs, German style, turn a bowl of meat soup or even brown stock into a complete winter meal. You can poach eggs in clear soups (remove them with a draining spoon and trim the whites into neat rounds if you wish) and there is

Fish Kebabs (page 6) ; Bacon Kebabs (page 8) ; Sausage Kebabs (page 9) ;
Friar's Omelette (page 10)

another meal in a garnish. Serve the eggs only lightly cooked so that the yolk breaks in the soup.

Jellied soups, which are actually more like salads than broths, are always sharpened with a squeeze of lemon juice and look attractive if decorated with extra twists of lemon. Crisp sprigs of fresh watercress or wafer-thin slices of tomato soften the cube-like appearance of the soup and offer a lighter texture.

Prepare the garnish in advance—the parsley ready chopped, the egg yolks sieved or chopped, the croûtons made—but always sprinkle them on to the soup just as you bring it to the table. Do not allow the garnish time to sink to the bottom of the bowl, melt in the heat of the soup, or become soggy. Once it becomes part of the soup itself, most of its purpose is lost.

Croûtons

thick slices of white bread, crusts removed
butter for frying

Cut the bread into fingers and then into cubes. Melt the butter to smoking point in a heavy frying pan and drop in the bread cubes, a few at a time. Turn them over to brown them on all sides. Remove with a draining spoon and drain on crumpled kitchen paper.

When they are thoroughly dry, you can store them in an airtight container. To give the garnish more flavour, you can add some thoroughly crushed cloves of garlic to the butter when frying. The bread will absorb the flavour and impart it to the soup. Or you can first dip the cubes in milk, lift them out with a draining spoon and turn them in finely-grated cheese before frying in butter.

Cheese Straws

50 g (2 oz) butter
50 g (2 oz) flour
50 g (2 oz) fresh breadcrumbs,
finely grated

75 g (3 oz) cheese, finely grated
salt and cayenne pepper
little egg yolk to mix, if needed

Rub the butter into the flour and breadcrumbs until it is thoroughly blended. Add the cheese and season with salt and cayenne pepper (use this sparingly). Mix together with your fingertips and add a little beaten egg yolk if needed to bind the mixture to a smooth paste. Roll out on a lightly-floured board to 0·5 cm (¼ in) thick and cut into fingers. Re-roll the pastry trimmings and cut some in circles, using 2 sizes of pastry cutter. Place on a greased baking sheet and bake at 190°C (375°F)/Gas 5 for 10–15 minutes, until golden brown. To serve, push the straws through the rings. Serve hot or cold.

Jellied Madrilène (page 20) ; Lentil Soup (page 23)

Cheese Scones

225 g (8 oz) flour
¼ teaspoon bicarbonate of soda
1 teaspoon cream of tartar
50 g (2 oz) butter
100 g (4 oz) grated cheese

salt and cayenne pepper
¼ teaspoon dry mustard
about 125 ml (scant ¼ pint) milk
little beaten egg, to glaze

Sieve the flour, bicarbonate of soda and cream of tartar together into a bowl and rub in the fat. Stir in most of the cheese, reserving a little for the tops, and season with salt, a pinch of cayenne pepper and the mustard. Pour in enough of the milk to form a soft dough. Turn on to a floured board and knead until the dough is free from cracks. Roll out to about 2·5 cm (1 in) thick and cut into small squares, then diagonally in half to form triangles. Place on a greased baking sheet, glaze with a little beaten egg and milk, sprinkle with the remaining cheese and bake at 220°C (425°F)/Gas 7 for about 10 minutes until the tops are golden brown.

Dumplings

175 g (6 oz) flour
1½ teaspoons baking powder
½ teaspoon salt
pinch of grated nutmeg

freshly-ground black pepper
40 g (1½ oz) white fat
cold water to mix

Sieve the flour, baking powder, salt and nutmeg together into a bowl, and add a few grindings of black pepper. Rub in the fat and add enough cold water to give a firm dough. Divide the mixture into 24 walnut-sized balls and drop into a meat soup or brown stock for 20 minutes before serving. The dumplings will sink to the bottom of the pan at first, but after a few minutes they will lighten and rise to the top.

You can vary this recipe endlessly, adding a few pinches of caraway or cumin seed, a pinch of mixed herbs or any dried herbs that complement the soup, or you can increase the proportion of spices, and add others.

Melba Toast

I have often heard guests in restaurants ask how melba toast is made. Why does it look so difficult, when it's really so easy?

Cut very thin slices of stale bread, or use sliced wrapped bread. Lay the bread on baking sheets and dry in the bottom of a very slow oven—the warm oven of a two-oven cooker is ideal. Now here is the secret—before serving the toast, brown the slices under a very low grill or, if the oven is on, at a moderate heat for just a few minutes.

DRIED BEANS AND PEAS

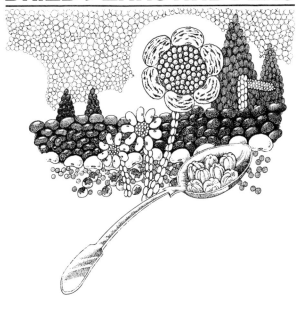

There's no food in the world that keeps longer in perfect condition than the colourful, exciting range of dried beans and peas. Huge earthenware pots of them have been dug up recently, a legacy hoarded by civilisations thousands of years ago, and the contents found to be as wholesome and nourishing as the day they were stored.

In those days, in Greek and Roman times, dried beans played the vital part of the ballot paper in political elections. A white bean signified a vote in the affirmative, an 'aye', while a black bean was cast as a signal of disapproval. But with beans and peas ranging in size from large marbles to little more than pin-heads, and in colours that would do credit to a shelf full of boiled sweets in a sweetshop, round the dinner table a vote of no-confidence is out of the question!

Dried beans and peas do not represent an instant food, the kind of store you can draw on at a moment's notice when a friend turns up on the doorstep unexpectedly. But what they do offer is the chief ingredient, still economical even now, for a whole range of aromatic, delicious, peasanty casseroles—soups, too—that you can cook slowly and surely for tomorrow.

Long, slow cooking is the secret of all these dried vegetables; indeed many of them have a tendency to burst and break under fierce heat. And there is another secret. *Never* add the salt until the final few minutes of the cooking time. (Lentils and split peas are the only exception.) Salt added at the beginning toughens up the beans and peas; at the best, they will take far longer to cook before they become tender, and in more obstinate cases they just never will. This is a simple tip but so worth remembering, especially for the many cooks who are inclined to add a pinch of salt to everything, right at the outset. If it's more convenient, stir in the salt just before serving, and then let the pot stand for a minute or two while the flavour is absorbed.

In general, all dried beans and peas require soaking for about six hours, or overnight, before they are strained and cooked. A pinch of bicarbonate of soda added to the water helps to soften them. *Never* soak them for longer than about eight hours, though, because they will start to ferment and germinate. It is usually best, then, to put them in fresh cold water, bring it slowly to the boil, and simmer for the amount of time suggested for each type of vegetable in the list below. Where this general method varies, other instructions are given. Dried beans and peas swell to between two and two-and-a-half times their volume after soaking, so it is important to allow them this amount of room to expand and enough water to absorb. If you fill them to the top of a small container and leave them overnight, you are likely to step on them all over the kitchen floor the next morning! And if you cook them before they have absorbed enough water, they will continue to take up the cooking liquid and cause the dish to dry out.

The cooking times given for individual beans and peas are those at which the vegetables will become just tender and succulent, without collapsing. Serve them as a vegetable accompaniment, with butter and a garnish of fresh chopped herbs and plenty of ground black pepper. They make an interesting and nutritious addition to many everyday dishes. If you are putting the beans or peas in a casserole or other recipe, follow the times specified in the recipe you are using.

When you are cooking beans separately, cook an extra handful for a salad. Strain these, allow them to cool thoroughly and serve them as an original and tasty opening course or a salad accompanying a meat or fish dish, on a bed of lettuce or raw spinach leaves. Use a good vinaigrette or oil and lemon dressing and scatter fresh chopped parsley over the beans.

Because these dried vegetables profit from patient, gentle cooking they are ideal partners for cheaper cuts of meat, boiling fowl or root vegetables, and this is the way in which they are used in most of the recipes that follow.

Use whatever method of long, slow cooking is the most economical for the appliances you have. If you have a solid fuel or oil-fired cooker, simmer the vegetables overnight or all day long in the low-heat oven; and for extra economy you can plan to cook meringues, or heat a dish of stoned fruit to soften slowly at the same time. To cook the larger types of dried vegetables, such as butter beans or chick peas, in an electric slow cooker, it is an advantage first to boil them in a saucepan of water for about 30 minutes. For on-the-hob cooking, set an asbestos mat under the pan or casserole and have the heat as low as possible, allowing the liquid just to turn over gently at simmering point, and stir occasionally with a wooden spoon to redistribute the contents of the pan. Pressure cooking comes into its own with the dried vegetables that need the longest cooking time and produces plump, perfect beans and peas.

The range of dried beans and peas we can buy has increased enormously in recent years. Enthusiastic cooks no longer have to be as adventurous and inventive as possible with just butter beans, haricot beans and the red kidney ones that are the basic stand-by of chilli con carne. Supermarkets now stock an interestingly wide variety, and the health food shops add still more with exotic names and subtle, unusual flavours.

In all of the following recipes, be prepared to experiment with beans and peas other than the ones specified. Follow the soaking and cooking times for the ones you use (which might be slightly different) and you can invent a whole new repertoire of warming dishes.

Many types of beans and peas which are available in packets have been pre-soaked. Always check on the label to see if this is so. Perhaps one or two kinds are a good stand-by for the times when you cannot plan far enough ahead, but you usually have to pay a fairly high price for this small convenience. Others, available in cans, have been not only pre-soaked but cooked; canned red kidney beans for immediate action in a dish of chilli con carne, for example, can be a good store-cupboard regular.

Aduki beans

Small, round brick-red beans with a white 'flash'. They have a sweet flavour which blends particularly well with pork, duck or goose. Soak them in cold water for 5–6 hours or overnight (maximum 8 hours), discard any that float to the top, then drain. Put them in a pan with 3 parts of warm water—say, 1 cup of beans and 3 cups of water—and bring slowly to the boil. Lower the heat, cover and simmer for 1 hour or until soft. Stir in salt just before serving and leave for a minute or two while the beans absorb the flavour.

Black beans

Sometimes called turtle beans. They are small and oval with black skins, but are white inside. These beans are used extensively in South American and Mexican cooking and, consequently, have a rather exotic reputation here. Soak them in cold water overnight (maximum 8 hours), discard any floating ones, strain, then simmer for 2–3 hours. Black beans are particularly good in dishes which include plenty of onion, with red and green peppers, and with boiled ham.

Black-eyed beans

Small, oval white beans (called black-eyed peas in some parts of America), with a black spot, like a dark pupil in an eye. Soak for about 6 hours, then simmer for $1\frac{1}{2}$–2 hours. Very good with lamb and with spiced sausages.

Butter beans

One of the most widely available types of pulses in the U.K., butter beans are a welcome familiar ingredient in soups, stews and casseroles. They are kidney-shaped, large, flat and cream-coloured. Soak them overnight (maximum 8 hours), then simmer for about 3 hours. Fast cooking causes the outer skin to break away and spoils the appearance of the dish.

Chick peas

Known as *garbanzoes* in Spain and Portugal, *revithia* in Greece. A favourite

42

ingredient of many Mediterranean country dishes of salt pork, tomatoes and even fish. Chick peas are about the size and shape of small, shelled hazelnuts. In Greece and some Eastern countries ground, cooked peas are mixed to a smooth paste with olive oil and herbs and served as an appetiser (houmus), with steaming hot slices of flat bread, or mixed with herbs, lemon and beaten egg to form flat rissole cakes, to be served with tomato sauce. Try these ideas with any left-over cooked peas. First soak them overnight (maximum 8 hours), with a large pinch of bicarbonate of soda added to the water, then simmer for $2\frac{1}{2}$–3 hours. It is particularly important to observe the no-salt-until-the-end rule, or the peas will harden irreversibly.

Fava beans
Similar to lima beans, but round, fava beans are probably the most piquant of all, with a distinctive sharpness. If you do not like this 'tang', add a pinch of sugar to the dish to offset it; used sparingly, the sugar will not mask other flavours. After soaking for up to 6 hours, cook the beans for about 1–$1\frac{1}{2}$ hours. Use them in poultry dishes.

Flageolets
The pale green seeds of haricot beans, flageolets are looked upon as the king among dried beans. After soaking for $1\frac{1}{2}$–2 hours, simmer for $\frac{3}{4}$–1 hour. Cooked dried beans, put through a sieve or blended in an electric blender, make a very good vegetable purée; served cold, and whole, they make a very good salad with a vinaigrette dressing.

Gungo peas
You can sometimes find these dried peas in health food shops; otherwise, track them down in West Indian or West African food specialist shops in a large town. They are small and dull brown in colour. Soak for about 6 hours, then simmer for $2\frac{1}{2}$–3 hours. Very good in mixed vegetable dishes.

Haricot beans
The most widely known haricot beans, the seeds of dwarf beans, are pale milky white, like fat little miniature versions of butter beans, though there are other varieties which are purple, red, brown or green. After soaking for $1\frac{1}{2}$–2 hours, simmer for 2–3 hours. These beans are the main ingredient of cassoulet, the classic French country dish, and complement all kinds of meat and poultry.

Lentils
Lentils, alone among the dried bean and pea family, should not be stored for a long time: after a few weeks they harden and refuse to become succulent, even with the longest, slowest cooking. There are three main types: the

43

popular orange-coloured ones which are grown in the Middle East; the yellow ones, the produce chiefly of European farms; and the dark browny-green ones which are sometimes called German lentils. The properties of each type are similar and so they are interchangeable in recipes. Soak lentils for about 3 hours, or overnight (maximum 8 hours), discarding discoloured ones or any that float to the top. Cook them in the same water. Bring it slowly to the boil, then simmer for about $\frac{1}{2}$ hour or, for German lentils, about $\frac{3}{4}$–1 hour. Salt *may* be added at the beginning of cooking. Specially good with bacon or ham. To make lentil purée, rub them through a sieve to remove the hard outer skin.

Lima beans
Similar to haricot beans, limas have green or white flat, kidney-shaped seeds which vary in size according to the particular type. After soaking for $1\frac{1}{2}$–2 hours, simmer for $\frac{3}{4}$–1 hour.

Mung beans
A most attractive, deep olive green, these small round beans can be bought now in most health food shops. When cooked, they are almost as bright as fresh green peas, and make a colourful addition to stews and soups. After soaking for about 6 hours, simmer for $\frac{3}{4}$–1 hour.

Peas, split
The peas always split during the drying process (a different variety is used to produce whole dried peas). Being half the size, split peas take less time to cook. Add a good pinch of bicarbonate of soda to the water, soak for about 6 hours or overnight (maximum 8 hours) and discard any that are discoloured or float to the top. Cook for about $\frac{3}{4}$–1 hour. You may add salt at the beginning of the cooking time.

Peas, whole
Many people still prefer the flavour and texture of dried peas to canned ones. Soak dried peas overnight (maximum 8 hours) in warm water. Add $\frac{1}{2}$ teaspoon bicarbonate of soda to each 225 g ($\frac{1}{2}$ lb) of peas. Bring slowly to the boil in fresh cold water and simmer for $2\frac{1}{2}$ hours.

Pinto beans
Often the most attractive of dried beans, they are pink speckled with brown. Although their flavour blends well with tomato and onion mixtures, it seems a shame to cloak the vivid colour in a red sauce. They are also good in mixed vegetable dishes. After soaking for about 6 hours, simmer for about 2 hours.

Red kidney beans
The basic and familiar ingredient of chilli con carne and a good accompaniment to beef and minced beef. Soak them overnight (maximum 8 hours), then simmer for at least 1½ hours. Add plenty of salt before serving.

Soya beans
Not immediately recognisable, since they vary in colour and can be yellow, green, brown or black. They are a well-known source of protein and, unlike some other beans and peas, contain very little starch, a plus factor for weight-conscious cooks. Soak for about 6 hours, then simmer for 2½–3 hours. Soya beans blend well with all kinds of meat and poultry.

Butter Bean Hot-pot

Butter beans and root vegetables form an interesting partnership in this warm winter casserole. It is ideal for cooking in an electric slow cooker; at such a low temperature it will become even more delicious.

100 g (4 oz) butter beans, soaked
50 g (2 oz) butter
1 large onion, peeled and chopped
225 g (8 oz) potatoes, peeled and sliced
175 g (6 oz) carrots, peeled or scraped and sliced
3 large tomatoes, skinned and sliced (or a small can of tomatoes, sliced)
1 small swede, peeled and sliced (optional)
100 g (4 oz) large mushrooms, wiped and sliced
1 large leek, washed and sliced
1 small can tomato purée
600 ml (1 pint) liquor in which butter beans were cooked (or you can use chicken stock)
salt and freshly-ground black pepper

Cook the soaked butter beans for about 1 hour. Drain and reserve the liquor. Melt the butter in a frying pan and sauté the chopped onion until soft but not brown. Grease a large casserole and scatter a layer of the onion in the bottom and then arrange layers of the vegetables, alternating the root vegetables with the 'soft' ones—the beans, tomatoes, mushrooms and leek. Put a little onion mixture between each layer and season well. Reserve some potatoes to overlap in neat rings to form a lid on top. Mix the tomato purée into the reserved liquor and pour into the casserole. It should not come more than 1 cm (½ in) from the top. Cover the casserole, stand on a baking sheet, and bake in a slow oven 110°C (225°F)/Gas ¼, for 2½ hours, removing the lid for the last ½ hour. (In a slow cooker, there is no point in removing the lid.)

You can prepare several dishes for the freezer, ringing the changes on the topping—creamy mashed potatoes with cheese are a good alternative.

Serves 4–6

Revithia Casserole

I first tasted this dish on a Sunday morning in Greece, when an old lady gave me a cupful, steaming hot, in the street. She had sent her huge, blackened casserole by bus to the next village, where it had simmered overnight on the embers of the baker's oven. I asked her what meat had given the peas such flavour and was surprised to be told there wasn't any.

350 g (12 oz) chick peas, soaked
 with a large pinch of bicarbonate of
 soda
2 tablespoons olive oil
1 large onion, peeled and sliced
2 large cloves garlic, peeled and
 crushed
2 stalks celery, washed and thinly
 sliced

1 large green pepper, trimmed and
 thinly sliced
1 heaped teaspoon dried basil
1 tablespoon fresh chopped parsley
225 g (8 oz) tomatoes, skinned and
 sliced
salt and freshly-ground black pepper

Drain the soaked chick peas and simmer in water for about 1½ hours. Melt the oil in a flameproof casserole, add the onion, garlic, celery and pepper and sauté until soft but not browning. Add the herbs, stir well and add the tomatoes and drained chick peas. Season well and stir to blend. Cover tightly with foil under the lid so that no moisture escapes, and bake at 130°C (250°F)/Gas ½ for 2½ hours.

Serves 4

Fruit and Bean Pot *(photograph facing page 52)*

There's no end to the versatility of haricot beans—without a very strong flavour of their own they are ready to take on interesting combinations of meat, fruit and vegetables. This recipe, which includes apples and prunes, makes a talking-point dish that would delight the most discerning supper guests. It is ideal for cooking in an electric slow cooker.

225 g (8 oz) haricot beans, soaked
225 g (8 oz) meat from knuckle end
 of bacon, soaked
350 g (12 oz) potatoes, peeled and
 thickly sliced
225 g (8 oz) prunes, soaked

350 g (12 oz) fresh dwarf or runner
 beans, cut into 2·5-cm (1-in) strips
salt and freshly-ground black pepper
450 g (1 lb) firm cooking apples,
 peeled, cored and thickly sliced

Put the soaked beans into a pan, remove the rind from the bacon, cut into chunks and add to the pot. Cover with cold water. Bring slowly to the boil, then simmer for 1½ hours. Add the potatoes, prunes and fresh beans, a little more water if necessary, and season with salt and pepper. Stir well and simmer very slowly for a further 15 minutes. Add the apples and continue to simmer until they are tender but not breaking—about another 15 minutes. Serve with hot, crisp bread.

Serves 4

Greek Lenten Family Supper

The addition of noodles to a dish of lentils would not normally be my first choice, especially if I were entertaining weight-watchers. But, as with so many unlikely culinary partnerships, this traditional Greek Lenten dish has an interesting contrast of textures and blend of flavours. And you can always have a salad day tomorrrow!

225 g (8 oz) green lentils, soaked
1 small can tomato purée
1 medium-sized onion, peeled and grated
1 large clove garlic, peeled and crushed

1 teaspoon dried basil
4 tablespoons good olive oil
900 ml–1·2 litres (1½–2 pints) water or chicken stock
225 g (8 oz) noodles
salt and freshly-ground black pepper

Put the soaked lentils into a pan, add the tomato purée, onion, garlic, basil, olive oil and water or stock. Bring slowly to the boil, then simmer for 15 minutes. Add the noodles and continue simmering for ¾ hour until the lentils and noodles are soft. (Note that this is a Greek recipe, and the addition of the olive oil and the water at the same time is their traditional method. They rarely sauté the onion and garlic in the oil first, as British cooks do.) Check from time to time that the dish is not drying out, and add a little more water if needed. Season well with salt and pepper.

Serve hot with a green salad or (if you are not observing a fast) with boiled ham.

Serves 4–6

Macaroni and Beans

If you can get used to the idea of beans with pasta, here is another Greek recipe which combines soya beans with wholemeal macaroni so subtly you can barely tell one ingredient from the other. I was served this dish at Eastertime with a salad of cold green beans (beans again!) in an olive oil and lemon dressing. And it was good.

4 tablespoons good olive oil
225 g (8 oz) soya beans, soaked
1 large onion, peeled and grated
2 large cloves garlic, peeled and
crushed
600 ml (1 pint) water, warm
1 small can tomato purée
1 tablespoon fresh chopped parsley
1 teaspoon dried basil

1 tablespoon green celery leaves,
chopped (optional)
salt and freshly-ground black pepper
225 g (8 oz) wholemeal macaroni
rings
25 g (1 oz) cottage cheese
pinch of cayenne pepper to garnish
extra fresh chopped parsley to
garnish

Put the olive oil into a flameproof casserole and add the soaked beans, onion, garlic and water into which you have stirred the tomato purée. Add the herbs and celery leaves if available, and stir to blend. Bring slowly to the boil, lower the heat and simmer gently for 2 hours. Season well with salt and pepper and add the macaroni rings. Stir them into the beans and continue to simmer for 40 minutes or until they are soft, adding a little more hot water if necessary.

The cooked dish is a deep reddish brown. Sprinkle the cottage cheese on top, add a pinch of cayenne pepper and a scattering of parsley.

Serves 4–6

Black and White Domino

So many traditional peasant dishes have an instinctive contrast of colour and texture, an interest that is sometimes called upon to compensate for the simplicity of the ingredients. This mixture of black beans and rice is a speciality of the sugar-growing regions of Cuba. The rice must be cooked separately, which does mean another pan, but the results are well worth the effort.

225 g (8 oz) black beans, soaked
450 ml (¾ pint) water
1 large onion, peeled and sliced
2 cloves garlic, peeled and finely
chopped
freshly-ground black pepper

salt
25 g (1 oz) butter
225 g (8 oz) long-grain rice
4 hard-boiled eggs, sliced
fresh chopped parsley to garnish

Put the beans in a pan with the water, add the onion and garlic and season well with pepper. Cover, bring slowly to the boil, then simmer for about 2 hours. If the beans start to dry, add a little more warm water. When they are tender, strain off any water, season with salt and stir in the butter.

Meanwhile, cook the rice in plenty of boiling, salted water for 10–12 minutes, then strain.

Serve the rice in a ring in a heated shallow dish with the beans piled in the centre. Garnish with rings of hard-boiled egg slices and chopped parsley.

Serves 4–6

Channa Dhal

Although not strictly a one-pot recipe, no chapter on dried beans and peas would be complete without dhal, a familiar accompaniment to meat and fish curries. It can be either mild or hot, or whatever strength you choose in between, according to the spices you use. This one is fairly hot.

100 g (4 oz) split peas, soaked
300 ml (½ pint) water, hot
½ teaspoon chilli powder
½ teaspoon turmeric
4 tablespoons cooking oil
1 medium-sized onion, peeled and
  chopped

1 large cooking apple, peeled, cored
  and roughly chopped
2 tablespoons fresh chopped parsley
  or green tops of celery leaves
1 teaspoon garam-masala
1 teaspoon salt
juice of ½ lemon

Discarding the split peas that are discoloured and those that float to the top, drain the peas and put them in the pan with the water, chilli powder and turmeric. Bring slowly to the boil, turn down the heat and simmer for about 1 hour. Check occasionally to ensure that the mixture has not dried out—it will if the heat is too high—and add a little more hot water if necessary. An asbestos mat on the hob, after the mixture has come to the boil, will help.

Pour the oil into a thick-bottomed frying pan, add the onion and fry gently until soft but not beginning to brown. Add the chopped apple, stir and fry for a further 1–2 minutes. Add the herbs, garam-masala and salt, and stir well until the ingredients are thoroughly mixed.

Add the vegetables to the dhal and stir well. Serve at once, with a squeeze of lemon juice, or reheat the following day, when the flavours will have blended together more thoroughly.

Serves 4

Boiled Beef with Pease Pudding

One of the most traditional British one-pot combinations, for which the pease pudding, in a cloth, is suspended in the broth while a round of beef simmers gently. The pudding can be cooked in other ways: steamed in a pudding basin and turned out for serving, cooked in a pan in a very slow oven, or on the stove at the lowest heat. But only in a cloth in the broth will it take up the delicious flavours of the meat and vegetables.

For the pudding:
225 g (8 oz) split peas, soaked
pinch of salt
25 g (1 oz) butter
1 egg, well beaten
freshly-ground black pepper
pinch of brown sugar

For the main dish:
1·2–1·35 kg (2½–3 lb) piece brisket
of beef, tied in a round
450 g (1 lb) carrots, scraped or
peeled and diced
1 small turnip, peeled and diced
1 large onion, peeled and sliced
2 stalks celery, washed and cut into
2·5-cm (1-in) lengths
1 bouquet garni
few black peppercorns
sea salt

Put the soaked, split peas into the centre of a scalded pudding cloth, add a pinch of salt and tie securely, leaving room for the peas to expand as they absorb the cooking liquor.

Put the meat and prepared vegetables into a large flameproof pot, cover with water and bring slowly to the boil, then simmer for about 20 minutes. Skim off any froth that comes to the surface. Add the bouquet garni, peppercorns and sea salt to taste. Suspend the pudding so that it is covered by the cooking liquor and replace the lid tightly to secure it by the ends of the cloth. Bring slowly to the boil again and simmer for 3–3½ hours.

Turn out the peas and push through a sieve with a wooden spoon or through a mouli foodmill. Add the butter, beaten egg, pepper and sugar and more salt, if necessary. Beat well with a wooden spoon. Rinse the pudding cloth and return the pea purée to it. Tie it tightly and suspend in the meat broth again, to simmer for a further ½ hour while the egg in the mixture cooks.

To serve, place the meat on a heated dish and pile the pease pudding round it. Serve the vegetables and some of the broth separately. Reserve the remaining liquor as a basis for soup or another casserole dish.

Serves 6

Sausage and Bean Soup

This is not the kind of soup with which to start an elegant meal. It is a hearty Spanish country dish, to be served in deep soup plates, with plenty of steaming hot bread. It makes an adventurous one-dish meal for a supper party—you could invite your friends to a 'spoon' supper instead of a 'fork' one!

225 g (8 oz) butter or haricot
beans, soaked
1 medium-sized onion, peeled and
finely chopped
1 large clove garlic, peeled and
finely chopped
100 g (4 oz) salt pork, rind
removed
1·8 litres (3 pints) water
225 g (8 oz) smoked ham
100 g (4 oz) black sausage

225 g (8 oz) strong garlic-flavoured
pork sausage (Spanish chorizo
sausage, if obtainable)
225 g (8 oz) pork chipolata
sausages
175 g (6 oz) potatoes, peeled and
diced
salt and freshly-ground black pepper
pinch of paprika pepper
1 tablespoon fresh chopped parsley
to garnish

Put the soaked beans into a large, heatproof casserole with the onion, garlic and pork, in one piece. Add the water, cover, and bring slowly to the boil. Skim off any scum and simmer for 1 hour before adding the ham, also in one piece (if you cut it in cubes at this stage, too much of the flavour will be drawn into the cooking liquor, and it will toughen). Cook for a further 1 hour then add the whole sausages and diced potatoes. Simmer for a further ½ hour, taste and then season—the amount of salt and pepper you will need will depend on the types of sausage you use. Remove the meat, cut the pork and ham into 2·5-cm (1-in) cubes, and slice the sausages into bite-sized pieces. Return the meat to the pot, reheat for a minute or two and serve piping hot, sprinkled with parsley. Any left-over broth can be served as a less substantial soup another time.

Serves 4–6

Boston Baked Beans

This is such a familiar dish that one might almost be forgiven for thinking that baked beans *grew* in cans! But make your own using haricot beans, sugar and treacle, and see what a grand dish it can be.

350 g (12 oz) haricot beans, soaked
2 medium-sized onions, peeled
100 g (4 oz) dark brown sugar
3 tablespoons black treacle or
molasses
1 teaspoon dry mustard

salt and freshly-ground black pepper
300 ml (½ pint) water, hot
2 cloves
1 bayleaf
350 g (12 oz) salt pork, scored

Put the soaked beans and one whole, peeled onion in a large flameproof casserole and cover them with water. Cover the pan, bring to the boil and simmer for 1 hour, then strain, discarding the onion (the beans will not, of course, be fully cooked by then). Mix together half of the sugar, all the treacle and mustard, season well with salt and pepper and stir in the hot water.

Return the strained beans to the large casserole (be sure it has a well-fitting lid). Add the sugar mixture, the remaining onion, stuck with the cloves and the bayleaf. Stir gently so that the beans are well mixed into the liquor. Lay the salt pork, rind side up, on top of the beans and press it gently down, leaving the rind still exposed. Cover with the lid (and with foil beneath if it does not fit too well) and bake at 120°C (250°F)/Gas ½ for 4½ hours. Remove the lid for the last ½ hour and sprinkle the remaining brown sugar over the pork rind.

To serve, carve the pork into thick slices and surround with beans. A green vegetable such as broccoli is a good accompaniment.

Serves 4

Portuguese Pork Pot

You find a number of dishes in the Algarve using black-eyed beans, not in a great proportion to the other ingredients, but as just one of a number of vegetables.

100 g (4 oz) black-eyed beans,
* soaked*
225 g (8 oz) salt pork, cut into
* 2·5-cm (1-in) cubes*
225 g (8 oz) black pudding, skinned
1 large onion, peeled and sliced
2 tablespoons olive oil
1 teaspoon ground cumin

pinch of grated nutmeg
freshly-ground black pepper
450 ml (¾ pint) chicken stock
* (see page 24)*
350 g (12 oz) white cabbage,
* washed and shredded*
salt

Put the soaked beans in a flameproof casserole with the cubes of pork, black pudding, onion, olive oil, cumin and nutmeg, and season well with pepper. Pour in the stock, cover and bring slowly to the boil. Simmer on the top of the stove, or cook in the oven at 180°C (350°F)/Gas 4, for 1 hour. Add the cabbage, stir gently to blend and season with salt. Simmer for a further 15–20 minutes until cabbage is still slightly crisp. Cut the black pudding into slices and return to the pot. Serve with buttered noodles.

Serves 4

South American Pork and Beans

The strongly-flavoured chorizo sausage, which you can buy at many delicatessen counters, gives the best flavour to this dish. If your local stores cannot oblige, substitute any good, firm garlic sausage or even ordinary sausages. In that case, double the amount of garlic called for in the list of ingredients.

Fruit and Bean Pot (page 46)

225 g (8 oz) red kidney beans,
  soaked
2 tablespoons olive or vegetable oil
1 large onion, peeled and chopped
2 cloves garlic, peeled and crushed
675 g (1½ lb) smoked belly of pork,
  rind removed
1 small can tomato purée
scant 600 ml (1 pint) chicken stock
  (see page 24)

1 bayleaf
¼ teaspoon dried oregano or basil
350 g (12 oz) chorizo sausage,
  skinned
1 whole canned pimento, cut into
  narrow strips
salt and freshly-ground black pepper
1 tablespoon fresh chopped parsley
  to garnish

Put the soaked beans in a pan, cover with cold water, bring slowly to the boil and simmer for 1 hour. Heat the oil in a large flameproof casserole, add the onion and garlic and sauté until transparent but not beginning to brown. Drain the beans and add them to the pan together with the pork, cut into 2·5-cm (1-in) cubes. Stir the tomato purée into the warmed chicken stock and pour into the casserole. Add the bayleaf and herbs, stir well, cover and simmer for 1 hour. Add the chorizo or other sausage, and the pimento, taste the stock and season well. Simmer for a further ½ hour, stirring once or twice. Remove the bayleaf, cut the sausage into slices and return to the dish. Sprinkle with chopped parsley and serve piping hot.

Serves 4

Chilli Con Carne

Red kidney beans, tomatoes, red peppers and chilli powder make this a fiery-looking dish. If you are not sure that you really enjoy the taste (and not just the thought) of a burning hot spice, add the chilli powder a little at a time and taste. Stop when you have gone far enough. If you do inadvertently add too much spice, stir some yoghurt into the sauce before serving, or hand some separately.

4 tablespoons vegetable oil
900 g (2 lb) topside of beef,
  trimmed and cut into 2·5-cm (1-in)
  cubes
2 large onions, peeled and chopped
2 large cloves garlic, peeled and
  crushed
1 teaspoon (or more to taste) mild
  chilli powder or chilli seasoning

1 teaspoon dried oregano
1 small can red pimento, drained
  and cut into strips
1 small can tomato purée
600 ml (1 pint) brown meat stock
  (see page 18)
350 g (12 oz) red kidney beans,
  soaked
salt

Heat the vegetable oil in a large, heavy flameproof pan, add the cubed meat and fry over a high heat to seal. Remove with a draining spoon and keep

Moroccan Chicken (page 67); Old-fashioned Rabbit Pie (page 73) 53

warm. Add the onion and garlic, lower the heat and cook until transparent. Add 1 teaspoon chilli powder and stir into the onion mixture, then add the herb and pimento. Stir the tomato purée into the stock, pour into the casserole and bring slowly to the boil. Return the meat, add the beans and bring back slowly to the boil. Taste the liquor. If you think it can take a little more chilli powder, blend some into 1 teaspoon of olive oil in a cup, mix to a smooth paste and stir into the casserole. Simmer for 1½–2 hours until the meat and beans are tender. Season well with salt. Serve with a green salad and hot French bread.

Serves 6

Spiced Chicken and Peas

The subtle use of spices in this dish gives a hint of curry, but not enough to discourage those who don't like it!

225 g (8 oz) chick peas, soaked	*½ teaspoon garam-masala*
2 tablespoons vegetable oil	*½ teaspoon turmeric*
1 medium-sized onion, peeled and finely chopped	*1 small chicken, chopped into 4 portions*
1 large clove garlic, peeled and crushed	*strained juice and grated rind of 1 lemon*
1 teaspoon ground coriander	*450 ml (¾ pint) water*

Put the soaked chick peas in a saucepan, cover with water and bring slowly to the boil. Cook for 1¼ hours, then drain. Heat the oil in a flameproof casserole, add the onion and garlic and sauté over a low heat until soft but not beginning to brown. Add the spices and stir well. Cook gently for 1–2 minutes to blend. Add the chicken joints and cook, turning occasionally, until they have taken up the colour of the spices. Add the lemon juice, rind, water and strained chick peas and stir well to blend. Cover, and bring gradually to boiling point. Turn down the heat or transfer to a moderate oven, 160°C (325°F)/Gas 3, to simmer for 1½ hours. Check occasionally and add a little more water if the dish is becoming too dry.

Serves 4

Spiced Chicken Pot

Cassoulet, the traditional French dish, can have ingredients as grand or as humble as the occasion demands, or you can afford. Few of us now can consign half a goose or a shoulder of lamb to the pot when, as in this recipe, far more economical cuts give such delicious results. But if you do feel like splashing out, adapt the dish to the meats you have, keeping the total weight the same.

350 g (12 oz) flageolets, soaked
225 g (8 oz) chorizo or other garlic sausage, skinned
1 large wing portion of chicken, cooked and skinned (or you can substitute goose or duck if you have it)
450 g (1 lb) middle neck lamb, cooked and weighed after boning (or you can use shoulder of lamb)

1 large onion, peeled
few sprigs fresh parsley
1 large tomato, skinned and sliced
100 g (4 oz) salt pork, cut into cubes
2 large cloves garlic, peeled and chopped
freshly-ground black pepper
50 g (2 oz) fresh white breadcrumbs

Put the beans in a flameproof casserole, just cover with water and bring slowly to the boil. Simmer for 1 hour. Add the sausage, chicken piece and lamb, the whole onion and the parsley. Bring slowly to the boil and simmer for a further 2 hours. Add the tomatoes, the cubes of pork and the garlic, and simmer for another 1½–2 hours.

With a draining spoon, remove the meats, take out the bones and cut the meat into bite-sized pieces. Return to the pot, season well with pepper and sprinkle the top with the breadcrumbs. Put the casserole in a very hot oven or, if it is more economical, under a medium-high grill, to brown the crumbs. Serve the dish with only a little of the liquor—it is not a soup. But any remaining can indeed be served as a soup at another time.

Serves 4–6

Farmhouse Lentil Fare

The deep greeny-brown lentils are the ones to make this country dish rich and rewarding. The orange lentils do not give such a good, crunchy texture.

25 g (1 oz) butter
175 g (6 oz) shallots, peeled
450 g (1 lb) boiled bacon, in one piece (reserve the stock)
2 cloves garlic, peeled and crushed
350 g (12 oz) brown lentils, soaked
1 large carrot, peeled or scraped

2 stalks celery, washed and cut in half
1 bouquet garni
about 600 ml (1 pint) stock in which the bacon was boiled
freshly-ground black pepper
25 g (1 oz) butter for garnish

Melt the butter in a heavy flameproof casserole, add the whole shallots and sauté until they are beginning to brown. Add the bacon, in one piece, and the remaining ingredients, except the pepper and butter. Simmer very gently for

2 hours. Check occasionally and if the dish shows signs of drying out, add more bacon stock, a little at a time.

The lentils should be tender but not mushy. When they are ready, remove the bacon and cut it into bite-sized chunks. Remove and discard the herbs, carrot and celery, which by now will have given their flavour to the lentils. Season the lentils well with pepper—remember none has been added so far— and gently stir in the butter. Make a ring of the lentils round the outside of a heated shallow serving dish and pile the bacon pieces in the centre. Serve with a crisp, green salad such as endive and chicory.

Serves 4

Mutton with Mung Beans

Few butchers admit to selling mutton now—everyone is supposed to want spring lamb. If you can buy mutton, the stronger flavour will improve the dish. If you can't, it will be good anyway.

4 tablespoons olive oil	*2 large tomatoes, skinned and*
about 550 g (1¼ lb) shoulder of	*sliced*
mutton or lamb, cut into 2·5-cm	*1 handful celery leaves, chopped*
(1-in) cubes	*350 g (12 oz) mung beans, soaked*
1 large onion, peeled and chopped	*freshly-ground black pepper*
1 large clove garlic, peeled and	*450 ml (¾ pint) chicken stock*
crushed	*(see page 24)*
1 teaspoon ground coriander	*salt*

Heat the oil in a flameproof casserole and add the meat, a few pieces at a time. Seal over a fairly high heat and remove with a draining spoon. Keep warm. Add the onion and garlic to the oil and sauté until just transparent. Stir in the coriander. Add the tomatoes, celery leaves, meat and soaked beans. Season with pepper and add the chicken stock. Bring slowly to the boil, lower the heat and simmer for 1 hour, or until the beans and meat are tender, then add salt. Check that the dish does not dry out; add a little more warmed stock if necessary. Serve with a green vegetable and fresh wholemeal bread.

Serves 4

Cream of Beans

Served in a lemon-flavoured cream sauce, soya beans take on a new elegance and make an interesting accompaniment to roast lamb or veal. (To make this recipe a meal in a pot, you can grill some sausages, stir them into the creamed vegetable and serve a new and delicious version of pork and beans.)

225 g (8 oz) soya beans, soaked   *150 ml (¼ pint) fresh soured cream*
50 g (2 oz) butter   *1 teaspoon strained lemon juice*
2 stalks celery, washed and chopped   *salt and freshly-ground black pepper*
pinch of grated nutmeg   *225 g (8 oz) pork chipolata*
450 ml (¾ pint) chicken stock   *   sausages, grilled*
* (see page 24)*

Put the beans in a flameproof casserole with the butter, chopped celery and nutmeg. Add the stock, bring slowly to the boil then simmer for 2½ hours. Add a little more warmed stock if necessary during this time. When the beans are tender and the stock has been absorbed, stir in the soured cream and the lemon juice and season well. Return to a low heat and stir to blend, but do not allow to boil.

To transform the beans into a supper dish, grill the pork chipolatas and stir them into the beans, or add some left-over cold meat. Serve with a small cottage loaf for a farmhouse meal.

Serves 4, as a vegetable or as a supper dish

CHICKEN AND RABBIT

Chicken, the luxury dish of our childhood, has to fight hard for first place in our affections today. It compares so very favourably, price-wise, with other meats, that we turn to it again and again for the sake of the budget.

Not only that, chicken is one of the quickest of meats to cook, so we can rely on it for all those occasions when we would like 25 hours in a day or an extra pair of hands to cope. If you have an hour from start to finish, you can cook a whole chicken in a variety of one-pot ways—as a traditional pot roast, with red pepper and tomato sauce, or with a sauce of vegetable purée, are just a few of the choices. Simplest of all, I like to sprinkle a whole chicken liberally with lemon juice and fresh tarragon, wrap it in foil with plenty of butter and cook it in a chicken brick at 200°C (400°F)/Gas 6. The smell becomes more and more tantalising as the hour progresses. In half an hour, you can cook chicken joints for four people and dress them up with unusual vegetable medleys, fruit, nuts and wine.

While the main dish is cooking you can toss together the ingredients for a crunchy topping. This may be as simple as buttered breadcrumbs, or dumplings, but it's a new texture, an added interest and more bulk to your one-pot meal.

Rabbit is one of my favourite meats, perhaps because we are lucky enough to be given one often, from nearby farms. But for these recipes, not wishing to cheat, I used frozen rabbit joints which usually, I find, take a little longer to cook. The cooking times given here are the minimum it will take for the meat to become tender. But longer, slower cooking is a good friend of rabbit and patient simmering, when you have time, will improve the texture of the meat and the depth of the sauce.

Chicken Complêt

For years I had roasted a chicken with the potatoes and then cooked a selection of vegetables separately—wasting fuel, time, energy and the chance to serve a meal as simply delicious as this one.

1 2-kg (4½-lb) roasting chicken
juice of ½ lemon, strained
salt and freshly-ground black pepper
1 onion, peeled and quartered
4 stalks celery, washed and cut into
  10-cm (4-in) sticks
4 carrots, peeled or scraped and
  halved lengthwise
50 g (2 oz) butter
550 g (1¼ lb) potatoes, peeled and
  quartered
300 ml (½ pint) water or chicken
  stock (see page 24)

For the lemon forcemeat balls
(optional):
50 g (2 oz) butter
1 small onion, peeled and finely
  chopped
75 g (3 oz) fresh white breadcrumbs
2 tablespoons fresh chopped parsley
grated rind of 1 large lemon
salt and freshly-ground black pepper
1 egg, beaten
1 tablespoon flour
25 g (1 oz) browned breadcrumbs

Wipe the chicken inside and out with a clean, damp cloth. Rub the lemon juice into the whole surface, dust liberally with salt and pepper and put the onion quarters inside the bird. Put the celery and carrot into the bottom of a large roasting pan with half the butter and place the chicken on top. Arrange the potatoes round the outside. Rub the remaining butter over the surface of the chicken. Season the potatoes with salt and pepper. Pour the water or stock into the pan, cover with household foil and roast at 190°C (375°F)/Gas 5 for ½ hour. Remove the foil. If you are making forcemeat balls, add them at this point. Roast the chicken for a further ½ hour, turning the forcemeat balls once to brown them on all sides. Remove the chicken to a warmed serving dish and arrange the vegetables and forcemeat balls round it.

To make the forcemeat balls, melt the butter in a small pan and sauté the onion until transparent. Remove from the heat. Stir in the breadcrumbs, parsley and lemon rind and season with salt and pepper. Bind with a little of the beaten egg. Roll the mixture into walnut-sized balls. Toss them in flour seasoned with salt and pepper, roll them in the remainder of the beaten egg and toss them in the browned breadcrumbs.

Serves 6

Chicken Brassica

The smooth sauce surrounding the chicken is a purée of vegetables in which crisp white cabbage is lightly cooked.

1 2-kg (4½-lb) roasting chicken	*750 ml (1¼ pints) chicken stock (see*
juice of ½ lemon, strained	*page 24)*
1 tablespoon olive oil	*pinch of sugar*
1 large onion, peeled and sliced	*salt and freshly-ground black pepper*
2 carrots, peeled or scraped and	*450 g (1 lb) firm white cabbage,*
sliced	*washed and cut into slices*
1 small parsnip, peeled and diced	*½ teaspoon caraway seeds*
2 tomatoes, skinned and quartered	*1 tablespoon fresh chopped parsley*
1 clove garlic, peeled and crushed	*to garnish*

Wipe the chicken thoroughly inside and out with a clean, damp cloth. Rub the meat with lemon juice. Put the olive oil and all the prepared vegetables into a large flameproof casserole, place the chicken on top and pour on the stock. Add a good pinch of sugar and season well with salt and pepper. Cover the casserole, bring the stock to the boil and simmer for 1 hour. Remove the chicken to a heated serving dish and keep warm. Put the vegetables and stock through a mouli mill, in an electric blender, or rub through a sieve. Taste the purée and add more seasoning if necessary. Return the purée to the pan and add the cabbage and caraway seeds. Simmer for 8–10 minutes until the cabbage is barely tender.

Remove the cabbage with a draining spoon and arrange round the chicken. Pour the vegetable purée over and sprinkle with chopped parsley to garnish. Serve with hot, crusty bread.

Serves 6

Chicken and Turnip Pot

Root vegetables (and an optional cheese topping) make a warm, wintry, homely meal of chicken legs.

4 chicken legs	*1 bayleaf*
1 tablespoon flour	*225 g (8 oz) fresh shelled peas (or*
salt and freshly-ground black pepper	*use frozen ones)*
50 g (2 oz) butter	
300 ml (½ pint) chicken stock (see	For the topping (optional):
page 24)	*6 slices white bread, without crust,*
4 small white turnips, peeled and	*buttered*
diced	*50 g (2 oz) cheese, grated*
225 g (8 oz) young carrots, scraped	
and sliced	

Toss the chicken legs in the flour seasoned with salt and pepper. Melt the butter in a flameproof casserole and lightly fry the chicken for a few minutes, turning to brown all sides. Add the stock, turnips, carrots and bayleaf, season well and bake at 190°C (375°F)/Gas 5 for 15 minutes. Add the peas and cook for a further 15 minutes until tender. Remove the bayleaf before serving.

To make the topping, lay the thickly-buttered bread slices on a baking sheet and sprinkle them with the cheese. Bake in the oven at the same time as the casserole, for ½ hour, when the bread should be crisp and the cheese golden brown. Cut the bread into bite-sized triangles and float on top of the casserole.

Serves 4

Chicken Cartwheel Casserole

The pasta wagon-wheels are cooked in simmering broth with the chicken and vegetables. How much more delicious than when they are cooked and served separately!

3 tablespoons olive oil
4 chicken joints, skinned
1 tablespoon flour
salt and freshly-ground black pepper
1 teaspoon dried tarragon or ½
teaspoon fresh chopped herb
1 large onion, peeled and sliced
1 clove garlic, peeled and finely
chopped
2 stalks celery, washed and chopped

3 carrots, peeled or scraped and
sliced
1 small red pepper, trimmed and
sliced
600 ml (1 pint) chicken stock (see
page 24)
100 g (4 oz) mushrooms, wiped and
sliced
175 g (6 oz) pasta wheels

Heat the oil in a large pan. Toss the chicken joints in the flour seasoned with salt, pepper and tarragon and fry over a medium heat, turning to brown on all sides. Add the onion and garlic, stir well, and fry for a further 2–3 minutes before adding the remaining prepared vegetables. Pour on the chicken stock and bring gradually to the boil. Simmer for 15 minutes, then add the mushrooms and pasta. Bring to the boil again and simmer for a further 15–20 minutes until the pasta is just tender.

Serves 4

Paprika Chicken

I call this an in-between dish, just spicy enough to be different but not so hotted-up that some people might not enjoy it.

1 tablespoon flour	*2 teaspoons tomato purée*
½ teaspoon salt	*600 ml (1 pint) chicken stock (see*
2 teaspoons paprika pepper	*page 24)*
¼ teaspoon cayenne pepper	*50 g (2 oz) mushrooms, wiped and*
4 chicken joints	*sliced*
25 g (1 oz) butter	*pinch of dried basil*
1 large onion, peeled and chopped	*1 bayleaf*
1 clove garlic, peeled and crushed	*soured cream to garnish*
1 red pepper, trimmed and sliced	*sprigs of parsley to garnish*

Put the flour, salt, paprika and cayenne pepper in a greaseproof or polythene bag and shake well. Toss the chicken joints one at a time to coat them with the seasoned flour. Melt the butter in a flameproof casserole and add the chicken pieces, to brown on all sides. Add the onion, garlic and red pepper and cook over a medium heat for 3–4 minutes. Stir the tomato purée into the chicken stock and pour into the casserole. Add the mushrooms, a pinch of dried basil and the bayleaf; stir well, until the tomato purée has blended in. Cover and bring to the boil. Simmer for 30–40 minutes until the chicken is tender. Remove the bayleaf. Shake teaspoons of soured cream on top of the chicken and garnish each one with a sprig of parsley. Serve with plain boiled rice.

Serves 4

Golden Chicken

Marinated in honey and decorated with peaches, this dish looks and tastes golden and summery. Serve it with a rice salad made colourful with chopped vegetables and fruit, or with plain boiled rice.

For the marinade:	*2 onions, peeled and sliced*
1 tablespoon clear honey	*1 green pepper, trimmed and sliced*
1 tablespoon cider vinegar	*2 tablespoons flour*
1 tablespoon soy sauce	*about 275 ml (scant ½ pint) dry cider*
4 tablespoons dry cider	*salt and freshly-ground black pepper*
	1 415-g (15½-oz) can peach halves,
4 chicken joints	*drained*
40 g (1½ oz) butter	*grated nutmeg to garnish*

Mix the honey, cider vinegar, soy sauce and 4 tablespoons dry cider together and pour in a shallow dish. Prick the chicken joints all over with a long darning needle, turn in the liquor several times and leave overnight to absorb the flavours. Strain the chicken and reserve the marinade.

Melt the butter in a flameproof casserole and brown the chicken joints on both sides. Lift them out with a draining spoon and set aside on a warm plate.

Sauté the onion and pepper for 2–3 minutes, then transfer to keep the chicken company. Shake the flour into the casserole and stir over a medium heat for 1–2 minutes until well blended. Pour the marinade into a measuring jug and make up to 300 ml (½ pint) with the cider. Gradually pour this on to the roux in the casserole, stirring until the sauce boils and thickens.

Return the chicken and vegetables to the casserole and stir carefully. Cover the casserole and cook at 190°C (375°F)/Gas 5 for about 1¼ hours until the chicken joints are tender. About 20 minutes before the end of the cooking time, add the peach halves to the casserole. Serve very hot, sprinkled with a little grated nutmeg.

Serves 4

Crunchy-topped Chicken

Buttered breadcrumbs make a crisp coating for the little herb balls which turn a simple chicken casserole into a meal-in-a-pot.

4 chicken joints
1 onion, peeled and chopped
1 large carrot, peeled or scraped and sliced
1 green pepper, trimmed and sliced
100 g (4 oz) mushrooms, wiped and sliced
about 275 ml (scant ½ pint) dry cider
salt and freshly-ground black pepper

For the topping:
40 g (1½ oz) butter
50 g (2 oz) fresh white breadcrumbs
225 g (8 oz) self-raising flour
1 teaspoon salt
freshly-ground black pepper
grated rind of ½ lemon
½ teaspoon dried oregano
2 tablespoons oil
little milk to mix
1 tablespoon fresh chopped parsley to garnish

Put the chicken joints, onion, carrot, green pepper and mushrooms in an ovenproof casserole, pour on the cider and season with salt and pepper. Cover and cook in the oven at 180°C (350°F)/Gas 4, for 15 minutes.

Meanwhile, make the topping. Heat the butter in a frying pan, add the breadcrumbs and fry until golden brown and dry. Set aside on a piece of greaseproof paper. Sift together the flour and salt and add the pepper, lemon rind and dried herb. Stir in the oil and add just enough milk to make the mixture soft and pliable. Shape into balls—you will need to flour your hands to do this—and roll in the buttered crumbs until thoroughly coated. Arrange the herb balls on top of the casserole in neat rings, turn the heat up to 190°C (375°F)/Gas 5, and bake uncovered for another 40–45 minutes. Sprinkle with chopped parsley to garnish.

Serves 4

Almond Chicken

Melting cheese and chicken do a great deal for each other. And in this recipe, the brown and crunchy toasted almonds complement both.

4 breasts of chicken, trimmed and
  skinned
1 tablespoon flour
salt and freshly-ground black pepper
½ teaspoon dried lemon mint or
  thyme
50 g (2 oz) butter
100 g (4 oz) button mushrooms,
  wiped and sliced

150 ml (¼ pint) dry white wine
3 tablespoons Marsala or sweet
  sherry
175 g (6 oz) Gouda cheese
40 g (1½ oz) blanched almonds,
  toasted until crisp and golden
  brown
1 teaspoon fresh chopped parsley to
  garnish

Toss the chicken breasts in the flour seasoned with salt, pepper and the dried herb. Melt the butter in a pan and sauté the chicken breasts for about 20 minutes, turning once, to brown both sides. Remove to a shallow flameproof serving dish and keep warm. Sauté the mushrooms for 2–3 minutes in the butter and remove with a draining spoon to the chicken dish. Sprinkle a very little flour in the pan and stir to 'set' any remaining butter and the meat juices. Pour in the wine, bring to the boil, stirring, and boil to reduce the volume by half. Pour the sauce over the chicken. Cut the cheese into thin slices and arrange over the chicken. Brown under a hot grill. Sprinkle first with the toasted almonds and then with the parsley to garnish. Serve with jacket potatoes and soured cream.

Serves 4

Chicken with Walnuts

Skillet, or frying-pan cooking, gives us the chance to prepare a main dish in the time it takes potatoes to boil. Here, the combination of mushrooms, walnuts and wine (either sneaked from the next or left-over from the last bottle) makes chicken joints fit for a party.

25 g (1 oz) butter
2 tablespoons oil
4 chicken breasts, trimmed
100 g (4 oz) mushrooms, sliced

50 g (2 oz) shelled walnut halves
4 tablespoons dry white wine
1 teaspoon fresh chopped parsley to
  garnish

Heat the butter and oil in a frying pan, or electric cook pan, and brown the chicken on both sides. Add the mushrooms, walnuts and wine and stir well. Cover the pan—with foil if you haven't a lid large enough—and simmer for 15–20 minutes. Lift out the chicken, mushrooms and walnuts with a draining spoon and arrange on a heated serving dish. Stir the juices in the pan and boil over a medium heat for 2–3 minutes to thicken. Spoon over the chicken and sprinkle with parsley to garnish.

Serves 4

Chicken Lasagne

A whole chicken is first cooked in one pot, to absorb the flavour of a sweet wine, then the meat sandwiched between layers of green lasagne to make an aromatic supper dish. Use quick-cooking lasagne to avoid an additional pan. You could assemble the dish in advance of a dinner party and heat it in the oven when the guests arrive.

4 tablespoons olive oil
50 g (2 oz) butter
1 large onion, peeled and chopped
3 cloves garlic, peeled and crushed
100 g (4 oz) streaky bacon, without rind, cut into small cubes
1 1·35-kg (3-lb) chicken, skinned
salt and freshly-ground black pepper

1 wineglass of sweet white wine or ·'cooking' sherry
450 g (1 lb) tomatoes, skinned and chopped
2 teaspoons dried basil
1 tablespoon fresh chopped parsley
350 g (12 oz) green quick-cooking lasagne
Parmesan cheese, grated, to serve

Heat the oil and butter in a large, heavy saucepan, add the onion and garlic and sauté over a medium heat for 4–5 minutes. Add the bacon cubes and fry until the fat runs, then put the chicken in the pan, turning it with 2 wooden spoons to brown lightly on all sides. Season with salt and pepper and pour in the wine. Cook, uncovered, until the liquid has evaporated, then add the tomatoes and herbs. Cover the pan and simmer for ½ hour, turning the chicken occasionally. Remove the chicken, cut the meat from the bones and return to the sauce.

Line the base of a well-buttered shallow ovenproof dish with lasagne 'leaves', cover with the chicken-sauce mixture and continue making alternate layers, finishing with the sauce. Bake at 180°C (350°F)/Gas 4 for 25 minutes. Serve with grated Parmesan cheese.

Serves 6–8

Moroccan Chicken *(photograph facing page 53)*

I have a few stand-by recipes I turn to over and over again for those occasions when visitors, perhaps on a weekday evening, arrive at the same time as we do. Oranges and lemons simmered with the chicken in a smooth yellowy sauce give this dish a sweet and sour effect.

1 tablespoon oil
2 onions, peeled and sliced
4 chicken joints, trimmed
1 teaspoon turmeric
600 ml (1 pint) chicken stock
(see page 24)

juice of 1 lemon, strained
salt and freshly-ground black pepper
1 tablespoon sugar
1 small orange, sliced, pips removed
1 lemon, sliced, pips removed
2 teaspoons cornflour

Heat the oil in a flameproof casserole and sauté the onion until transparent but not brown. Add the chicken joints and fry for 10 minutes, turning once to brown both sides. Stir in the turmeric and pour on the stock and lemon juice. Bring to the boil and season with salt, pepper and sugar. Add the orange and lemon slices and simmer for 15 minutes, until tender. Blend the cornflour with a little cold water and stir into the casserole, taking care not to break the fruit. Bring to the boil and simmer for 2 minutes. Serve with plain boiled rice sprinkled for colour with a little turmeric.

Serves 4

Orange Chicken

The flavours of the orange and Worcestershire sauce penetrate the chicken until it no longer tastes like a 'white' meat.

25 g (1 oz) butter
1 small onion, peeled and finely
   chopped
1 large orange
2 tablespoons Worcestershire sauce

1 teaspoon tomato purée
salt and pepper
4 chicken joints, trimmed
watercress sprigs to garnish

Melt the butter in a pan and sauté the onion over a medium heat for 5 minutes. Cut the orange in half. Pare the peel in thin strips from one half, removing any white pith which remains on the peel. Cut the peel into very thin matchstick strips. Finely grate the rind from the other half, and squeeze the juice from the orange. Add the orange strips, rind and juice, the Worcestershire sauce and tomato purée to the pan, stir well and season to taste. Bring the sauce to the boil. Cut 4 squares of household foil and place one chicken joint on each. Spoon over the orange sauce, turning each chicken piece so that it is well coated. Close up the foil parcels, sealing the joins well, and place in a shallow baking dish, join sides up. Bake at 200°C (400°F)/ Gas 6, for 30 minutes. Open the foil, baste the chicken pieces with the sauce and bake uncovered for a further 15 minutes until deep brown. Serve hot or cold, garnished with watercress.

Serves 4

Coriander Chicken Pilaff

Whole pieces of chicken are first marinated in lemon juice with coriander seeds, then served on a bed of herb-flavoured rice.

For the marinade:
1 tablespoon olive oil
juice of 1 lemon, strained
1 teaspoon coriander seeds, crushed
½ teaspoon salt
freshly-ground black pepper

4 chicken joints, skinned and
  trimmed

3 tablespoons olive oil
300 ml (½ pint) lager
300 ml (½ pint) chicken stock (see
  page 24)
275 g (10 oz) unpolished rice
3 tablespoons fresh chopped celery
  leaves
100 g (4 oz) frozen peas, thawed
salt and freshly-ground black pepper

Put the marinade ingredients into a shallow dish and stir well to blend. Prick the chicken pieces all over with a thick darning needle so that they more easily absorb the flavour. Put the chicken pieces in the dish, turn over to coat with the lemon mixture, cover and leave for about 5–6 hours, turning the chicken several times if convenient. Remove the chicken from the marinade, reserving the liquid, and pat dry.

Heat 3 tablespoons oil in a large flameproof casserole. Add the chicken and fry over a medium heat to brown all sides. Add the lager, chicken stock and strained marinade. Stir well, cover the casserole and cook for about 25–30 minutes until tender. Remove the chicken and keep warm. Add the rice to the casserole, and simmer for 15–20 minutes. Add the finely-chopped celery leaves and the peas and season with salt and pepper. Simmer for a further 5–10 minutes until the peas are tender.

Stir well with a fork and put the chicken pieces on top of the bed of rice. Allow to heat through, then serve from the casserole.

Serves 4

Cornish Casserole

The cider-cream sauce, sharpened by the inclusion of apple slices, is good with rabbit. Serve this dish with parsnips baked in the oven at the same time.

50 g (2 oz) butter
900 g (2 lb) rabbit joints
1 large onion, peeled and sliced
100 g (4 oz) button mushrooms,
  wiped and halved
25 g (1 oz) flour

300 ml (½ pint) dry cider
salt and freshly-ground black pepper
1 large cooking apple, peeled, cored
  and sliced
4 tablespoons single cream

Melt the butter in a flameproof casserole and fry the rabbit joints for a few minutes, turning them so that they brown on all sides. Lift the rabbit out with a draining spoon and keep warm. Sauté the onion and mushrooms in the remaining butter for 3–4 minutes, then remove them, too. Sprinkle the flour into the casserole, stir well and cook for 1 minute before gradually pouring in the cider. Bring to the boil, stirring, and season well. Return the rabbit and vegetables to the casserole, add the apple and stir to blend well. Cook in the oven at 180°C (350°F)/Gas 4, for $1\frac{1}{4}$–$1\frac{1}{2}$ hours, until the rabbit is tender. Stir in the cream just before serving.

Serves 4

Hunter's Stew

Rabbit is an economical meat, yet one which I always look upon as a treat. This casserole has a rich brown gravy—and, with the addition of snowball dumplings, is a meal in itself.

25 g (1 oz) butter	*For the dumplings:*
1 large onion, peeled and chopped	*4 rashers streaky bacon, without*
2 stalks celery, washed and chopped	* rind, chopped*
900 g (2 lb) rabbit joints	*100 g (4 oz) flour*
1 tablespoon flour	*$\frac{1}{4}$ teaspoon salt*
salt and freshly-ground black pepper	*40 g (1$\frac{1}{2}$ oz) shredded suet*
$\frac{1}{4}$ teaspoon dried thyme	*1 tablespoon fresh chopped parsley*
300 ml ($\frac{1}{2}$ pint) brown ale	*3–4 tablespoons water*
300 ml ($\frac{1}{2}$ pint) chicken stock (see	
* page 24)*	

Heat the butter in a large flameproof casserole and sauté the onion and celery over a medium heat for 5 minutes. Toss the rabbit pieces in flour seasoned with salt, pepper and dried thyme and fry in the casserole for 5 minutes, turning the meat to brown it on all sides. Add the ale and stock, stir well and bring to the boil, stirring occasionally. Cover and simmer over a low heat for 1 hour before adding the dumplings.

To make the dumplings, fry the bacon in a small pan until crisp. In a bowl, sift together the flour and salt, add suet, parsley, bacon and just enough water to mix to a soft dough. Shape into 8 balls. When the rabbit has been cooking for 1 hour add the dumplings to the casserole and simmer for a further 20–25 minutes. The dumplings will first sink into the liquor, then rise to the top, a light yet filling addition to the pot.

Serves 4

Rabbit with Raisins

Raisins soaked in wine, both in the sauce and as a garnish, bring a richness to fried rabbit.

2 tablespoons oil
50 g (2 oz) butter
900 g (2 lb) rabbit joints
1 tablespoon flour
salt and freshly-ground black pepper
6 shallots, peeled
50 g (2 oz) seedless raisins
150 ml (¼ pint) red wine

150 ml (¼ pint) chicken stock (see page 24)

For the garnish:
25 g (1 oz) raisins
2 tablespoons red wine
pinch of brown sugar

Heat the oil and butter together in a flameproof casserole. Trim the rabbit joints and toss them in the flour well seasoned with salt and pepper. Fry the rabbit for about 15 minutes, turning it so that it browns evenly on all sides. Add the whole shallots, raisins and red wine, bring to the boil, then add the chicken stock and bring to the boil again. Simmer for 35–40 minutes until the rabbit is tender.

Meanwhile soak 25 g (1 oz) raisins in 2 tablespoons red wine and a little brown sugar for the garnish. Sprinkle them over the casserole just before serving. Serve with potato purée or very soft mashed potatoes.

Serves 4

Red Spiced Rabbit

Think ahead to tomorrow and marinate rabbit joints in wine. The effect will be subtle but decidedly noticeable. Croûtons are a good crunchy garnish.

For the marinade:
1 large onion, peeled and chopped
2 bayleaves
300 ml (½ pint) dry white wine

675 g (1½ lb) rabbit joints
50 g (2 oz) butter
100 g (4 oz) streaky bacon, without rind, chopped
25 g (1 oz) flour
150 ml (¼ pint) chicken stock (see page 24)

1 tablespoon redcurrant jelly
¾ teaspoon red pepper sauce
100 g (4 oz) button mushrooms, wiped and sliced
salt

For the croûtons:
6 thick slices of bread, without crust
50 g (2 oz) butter
1 teaspoon dried mixed herbs

Mix together the marinade ingredients, and put them in a shallow dish with the rabbit joints. Turn them occasionally in the liquor and leave to absorb the flavours overnight. Remove the rabbit with a draining spoon and reserve the marinade.

Melt the butter in a flameproof casserole and fry the rabbit to brown it on all sides. Transfer it temporarily and keep warm. Strain the onion from the marinade and sauté this in the casserole with the bacon for 3–4 minutes. Sprinkle on the flour and cook, stirring, for 1 minute. Gradually pour on the reserved marinade and the stock and bring to the boil, stirring. When the sauce begins to thicken, add the redcurrant jelly and pepper sauce, and stir well to melt and blend in the jelly. Return the rabbit to the casserole and add the mushrooms. Taste and season with salt. Cook in the oven at 180°C (350°F)/Gas 4, for $1\frac{1}{4}$–$1\frac{1}{2}$ hours, until the rabbit is tender. Remove the bayleaves and serve garnished with herb croûtons.

To make the croûtons, cut the bread slices into cubes. Melt the butter in a frying pan, add the bread cubes and sprinkle with the dried herb. Fry until the bread is crisp and dry.

Serves 4

Mustard Rabbit

Not long ago someone called on us unexpectedly one Sunday. He was on his way to Bahrein and, knowing that I had an ample pot of rabbit simmering on the stove, I asked him to stay for a farewell lunch. 'Whatever that was, it was delicious,' he declared. 'I know it wasn't rabbit, because that's the one meat I can't eat!'

For the marinade:	1 tablespoon oil
150 ml ($\frac{1}{4}$ pint) dry cider	50 g (2 oz) butter
1 tablespoon oil	900 g (2 lb) rabbit joints
2 shallots, peeled and halved	2 tablespoons flour
$\frac{1}{4}$ teaspoon dried thyme	300 ml ($\frac{1}{2}$ pint) chicken stock (see
salt and freshly-ground black pepper	page 24)
1 bayleaf, crushed	1 tablespoon Meaux mustard
6 juniper berries, crushed (optional,	150 ml ($\frac{1}{4}$ pint) fresh soured cream
but important)	

Put all the marinade ingredients together in a small pan and bring to the boil. Pour into a shallow dish and, when cool, marinate the rabbit joints in the mixture, turning occasionally. Leave overnight if possible. Strain the rabbit and reserve the marinade.

Heat the oil and butter together in a large flameproof casserole and fry the rabbit to brown it on all sides. Lift out the rabbit and set it aside to keep warm. Stir in the flour, cook for 1 minute, stirring, and gradually pour in the strained marinade and the chicken stock. Bring the sauce to the boil, then stir in the mustard. Taste and season the sauce. Return the rabbit to the casserole, stir carefully to cover it with the sauce and bake at 170°C (325°F)/ Gas 3, for 1¼ hours, until the meat is tender. Stir in the soured cream and reheat without boiling. Serve with new potatoes.

Serves 4

Old-fashioned Rabbit Pie *(photograph facing page 53)*

This is the kind of one-pot dish to give to people who complain that things aren't what they used to be. Prove to them that in the kitchen, at least, old standards still remain.

For the marinade:
150 ml (¼ pint) red wine
4 tablespoons olive oil
2 sprigs parsley
1 bayleaf, crushed
¼ teaspoon dried thyme
2 shallots, peeled and sliced
1 clove garlic, peeled and halved

For the filling:
225 g (8 oz) prunes, stoned
675 g (1½ lb) boned rabbit, sliced
1 tablespoon oil
175 g (6 oz) belly of pork, without rind, cut in small cubes
2 rashers of bacon, without rind, chopped

2 medium-sized onions, peeled and sliced
50 g (2 oz) mushrooms, wiped and sliced
1 tablespoon fresh chopped parsley
salt and freshly-ground black pepper
large pinch of mixed spice
150 ml (¼ pint) well-reduced chicken stock (see page 24)

For the pastry:
175 g (6 oz) flour
½ teaspoon salt
40 g (1½ oz) butter
40 g (1½ oz) lard
little cold water to mix

Mix together the marinade ingredients, pour them into a shallow bowl and steep the prunes and rabbit slices in them overnight. Next day, melt the oil in a frying pan and fry the belly of pork, bacon and onion over a moderate heat for about 5 minutes, until the fat has run from the meat. Add the mushrooms and continue cooking for 1 minute. Strain the rabbit and prunes, reserving the marinade, and put the meat in a large bowl. Add the pork mixture and chopped parsley and season well with salt, pepper and mixed spice. Pour on the strained marinade and the stock.

Turn the meat mixture into a 1·8-litre (3-pint) pie dish and allow to cool.

To make the pastry, sift together the flour and salt and rub in the fats until thoroughly blended. Mix with a very little cold water to a smooth paste. Roll out the pastry and cut a 1-cm (½-in) strip from all round the edge. Grease the rim of the pie dish, press on the pastry strip and brush it with water. Lower the pastry on to the pie dish and trim and seal the edges. Make a hole in the centre of the crust. Re-roll the trimmings and cut leaves or other decorative shapes (I often use my apple corer, to stamp out crinkled circles). Brush the pastry with milk and arrange the decorations. Glaze them, too.

Stand the pie dish on a baking sheet and bake at 190°C (375°F)/Gas 5, for 1¼ hours. If the crust browns too quickly, cover it with foil towards the end of the cooking time.

Serve with a good old-fashioned green vegetable such as brussels sprouts. The pie is also excellent eaten cold.

Serves 6

Turkey Kebabs

Not so much a meal in a pot as a meal on a stick. Many food supermarkets sell turkey joints, which are ideal for cooking in this way. You can, of course, use chicken instead.

about 350–450 g (¾–1 lb) turkey meat
2 oranges
olive oil
12 stuffed green olives
50 g (2 oz) ham, cut in cubes
1 large green pepper, trimmed and cut in squares

For the marinade:
2 tablespoons olive oil
1 tablespoon red wine vinegar
grated rind of 1 orange
salt and freshly-ground black pepper
few cloves
pinch of nutmeg

Trim the turkey into neat bite-sized cubes and use any off-cut pieces in a soup. Grate the rind from 1 orange, to use in the marinade. Carefully peel both oranges and remove any remaining pith with a very sharp knife before dividing into segments. Brush 4 kebab skewers with olive oil and divide the turkey, orange segments, olives, ham and green pepper between them. Thread the ingredients to alternate the meats with the fruit and vegetables. Mix the marinade ingredients together. Put the threaded skewers on a shallow dish or large plate and brush with the marinade. Turn the skewers and baste with the marinade frequently. Leave for at least 2 hours before cooking.

Line the grill pan with household foil. Grill the kebabs under a high heat for about 10 minutes, turning them evenly and basting them frequently with the marinade. Serve them on a bed of plain boiled rice or speared into jacket potatoes.

Serves 4

74

LAMB AND PORK

Butchers used to say that no one wanted the cheaper cuts of meat, the scrag end or middle neck of lamb, belly of pork or streaky bacon rashers. But times have changed, and we all need a bank-load of recipes that don't cost a fortune, yet don't label us as church mice.

One-pot cooking is just made for the cheaper cuts. The long, slow cooking tenderises the meat and gives the sauce plenty of time to blend the flavours of the vegetables, fruit, herbs and spices we use for variety and interest.

Lamb has always been a favourite meat of mine. When I buy a joint for roasting, I always cut off a thick slice for a casserole dish—more interesting, I think, than serving the left-over meat cold. I love all the Middle Eastern ways with lamb, and so there are several here, casseroles tangy with fruit and spices, golden, glowing and delicious. And when there's a frost in the air, I unashamedly turn to the old ways, partnering not-too-elegant cuts of lamb from the freezer centre with good old-fashioned root vegetables and a topping of savoury dumplings.

Now that more and more of us buy our meat in bulk for the freezer, we are apt to find ourselves with several cuts we might not have chosen from the butcher. People often ask how to cook belly of pork, for instance, in interesting ways. After making pâté, and stuffing and rolling, what is there? A good lean piece can be used in most of the pork recipes here, substituted for the more expensive spare rib cut. If someone in your family is troubled by the richness and fat from pork, cook the dish the day before and lift off the layer of settled fat (be sure, then, to reheat the dish right up to boiling point), or skim the top carefully before serving. The addition of fruit—apples, pears, apricots or prunes—plays a subtle part in off-setting the richness, too.

Fennel Rack of Lamb *(photographed on the jacket)*

The lamb is threaded on dried fennel stalks, piercing the meat like wooden skewers and imparting all the scent of the wild herb in summer. You can buy packets of fennel in herb shops, or look out for some growing wild by the roadside. I found mine on an A road in Hertfordshire!

2 best ends of neck of lamb (12–14 chops)
4–6 stalks of dried fennel
4 tablespoons olive oil

For the stuffing:
25 g (1 oz) butter
1 medium-sized onion, peeled and finely chopped

1 clove garlic, peeled and crushed
1 green pepper, trimmed and chopped
3 stalks celery, washed and chopped
100 g (4 oz) fresh white breadcrumbs
1 teaspoon dried fennel leaves
salt and freshly-ground black pepper
1 egg, lightly beaten

To prepare the racks of lamb, trim away the meat and skin from the ends of the bones. Cut through the gristle that joins each chop. Place the 2 racks together with the bone ends interlocking, so that the joints form an X shape—rather like the fingers of your hands being crossed together. Tie the joint round with string to secure. Pierce through the meat with a skewer, then remove the skewer and push in the dried fennel stalks. Turn the joint upside down and pack with the stuffing. Stand upright in a roasting pan—I often use a deep oval pan with a high-sided lid—with the olive oil. Cover the tips of the bones with little squares of household foil to prevent them from burning. Roast at 180°C (350°F)/Gas 4, allowing ½ hour to each 450 g (1 lb) of meat, plus ½ hour extra. You can roast potatoes in their skins at the same time if you wish. To serve, remove the dried fennel stalks and the foil tips. Decorate the bones with prepared paper chop frills or with tiny tomatoes pierced by the bones. Cut the string before serving and allow 2–3 chops per person.

To make the stuffing, melt the butter in a small pan and sauté the onion and garlic for 3 minutes over a medium heat, then add the pepper and celery and cook for another 3 minutes. Add the breadcrumbs and dried herb leaves, season well with salt and pepper and bind with the beaten egg.

Serves 4–6

Envelopes of Lamb

This is a very good dish to cook on a barbecue if you want an outdoor meal to be more elegant than the sausage and hamburger kind. But it is equally good cooked in an oven, emerging all melting and gooey.

77

900 g (2 lb) slices lean lamb, cut from the leg	freshly-ground black pepper
juice of 1 lemon, strained	2 tablespoons olive oil
2 cloves garlic, peeled and crushed	100 g (4 oz) Gruyère cheese, thinly sliced
¼ teaspoon salt	4 sprigs of fresh rosemary

Place the slices of lamb in a shallow dish and marinate them in the lemon juice, garlic, salt and pepper mixed together. Brush the meat with the marinade until it takes it all up. Brush 4 squares of cooking foil with the oil and divide the slices of meat between them, covering each slice with a piece of cheese. Place a sprig of rosemary on each one and twist the foil to form a neat, tight parcel. Cook over a barbecue for 20–30 minutes, or in the oven at 180°C (350°F)/Gas 4, for 50 minutes. Cook jacket potatoes at the same time. Remove the rosemary sprigs and serve with the foil turned back, like water lilies.

Serves 4

Raan

The longer you leave the lamb steeped in the yoghurt and spices, the more tender and delicious the meat will be. I usually leave a whole joint for 48 hours or, when I adapt the dish to cook frozen lamb chops, thaw them in the marinade and leave them for 24 hours.

1 2·2-kg (5-lb) leg of lamb, trimmed of excess fat	1 teaspoon cardamom seeds
6 large cloves garlic, peeled and halved	12 cloves, split
	2 teaspoons turmeric
6 shallots, peeled and sliced	1 heaped teaspoon chilli powder
100 g (4 oz) fresh root ginger, scraped and sliced	1 tablespoon salt
	100 g (4 oz) ground almonds
juice and thinly-pared rind of 1 lemon	5 tablespoons soft dark brown sugar
	2 150-ml (¼-pint) cartons natural yoghurt
1 teaspoon cumin seeds	

Pierce the lamb joint all over with the sharp-pointed blade of a knife. Put the garlic, shallots, ginger, lemon juice and rind, spices and salt in an electric blender, and grind to a paste. If you do not have a blender, grind with a pestle and mortar. Spread the paste over the lamb to cover it completely and place in a deep plate for an hour or more. Blend the almonds together with half the sugar and the yoghurt. Spread this thick paste all over the lamb, cover it loosely with foil or greaseproof paper and leave in a cold place for up to 48 hours.

I always cook this dish in an earthenware 'chicken brick', which is ideal for this type of Indian clay cooking. But you can perfectly well use a covered roasting tin or an ordinary one covered with foil. Place the meat in the oven brick or roasting tin and roast, uncovered, at 220°C (425°F)/Gas 7, for $\frac{1}{2}$ hour, turning the meat once to seal it on all sides. Pat the remaining sugar all over the meat, turn the meat once more and cover the tin and lower the heat to 170°C (325°F)/Gas 3, for $3\frac{1}{2}$ hours, basting the meat with the sauce from time to time.

Transfer the meat to a heated serving dish and reduce the sauce by boiling over a high heat for 5–7 minutes. Pour a little of the sauce over the meat and serve the rest separately. Serve with plain boiled rice, grilled poppadoms and a selection of fruit chutneys.

Serves 6–8

Arabian Lamb

There's a strong bond between lamb and prunes—they're always delicious together and even more so with the combination of sugar and spice.

2 tablespoons cooking oil	*freshly-ground black pepper*
1 large onion, peeled and sliced	*1 tablespoon flour*
1 large clove garlic, peeled and crushed	*300 ml ($\frac{1}{2}$ pint) brown bone stock (see page 22)*
675 g ($1\frac{1}{2}$ lb) lean lamb, trimmed and cut into 2·5-cm (1-in) cubes	*2 bayleaves*
1 teaspoon turmeric	*1 heaped tablespoon soft dark brown sugar*
$\frac{1}{2}$ teaspoon ground cinnamon	*20 prunes, stoned, soaked overnight*
pinch of ground ginger	*in cold tea*
1 teaspoon salt	

Heat the oil in a flameproof casserole and fry the onion and garlic until they begin to soften. Add the meat and stir to brown the cubes on all sides, add the spices, salt and pepper. Sprinkle on the flour, stir well to blend thoroughly, and gradually pour in the stock, stirring until the sauce boils and thickens (the sauce blends better if you heat the stock first). Add the bayleaves, cover and cook at 180°C (350°F)/Gas 4, for 45 minutes. Stir in the sugar and strained prunes and continue cooking for a further 15 minutes. Remove the bayleaves before serving. Serve with plain, boiled rice.

Serves 4

Spiced Lamb

By mistake one day I took pork instead of lamb from my freezer, but pressed on regardless and found that this dish was just as successful, though doubtless less authentic.

675 g (1½ lb) meat, cut from leg of
  lamb
juice of 1 lemon, strained
1 tablespoon cooking oil
25 g (1 oz) butter
2 medium-sized onions, peeled and
  sliced
1 large clove garlic, peeled and
  finely chopped
1 tablespoon flour

¼ teaspoon ground cumin
¼ teaspoon ground allspice
¼ teaspoon turmeric
2 tablespoons tomato purée
300 ml (½ pint) white stock (see
  page 31)
salt and freshly-ground black pepper
1 teaspoon juniper berries, crushed
2 bayleaves, crushed

Trim the lamb, cut it into 2·5-cm (1-in) cubes and turn them in the lemon
juice. Pat them dry. Heat the oil and butter together in a flameproof casserole
and fry the meat, a few cubes at a time, stirring so that they brown on all sides.
Remove the meat with a draining spoon and set aside to keep warm. Add the
onion and garlic to the casserole and fry over a moderate heat until beginning
to soften. Tip in the flour and ground spices and stir well. Stir the tomato
purée into the stock and gradually pour into the casserole, stirring until the
sauce boils and thickens—it will blend better if you heat the stock before
adding it. Return the meat to the casserole and season well with salt and
pepper. Tie the crushed juniper berries and bayleaves in a piece of muslin
and push into the sauce. Cover the casserole and cook at 180°C (350°F)/
Gas 4, for 1–1¼ hours, until the meat is tender. Remove the muslin bag, and
serve the spiced lamb with buttered green noodles.

Serves 4

Honey Lamb Casserole

Marinating overnight in honey and cider does good things to lamb—like
accentuating the sweetness of the meat.

1 1·35-kg (3-lb) shoulder of lamb
2 tablespoons white wine vinegar or
  cider vinegar
1 tablespoon olive oil
1 tablespoon clear honey
½ teaspoon dried marjoram
4 tablespoons dry cider

15 g (½ oz) butter

1 medium-sized onion, peeled and
  chopped
2 medium-sized carrots, peeled or
  · scraped and sliced
100 g (4 oz) button mushrooms,
  wiped and quartered
40 g (1½ oz) flour
300 ml (½ pint) dry cider
salt and freshly-ground black pepper

Cut the meat from the bone and cut into 2·5-cm (1-in) cubes. Put the meat
cubes into a bowl with the vinegar, olive oil, honey, dried herb and cider, stir

well and leave in a cold place for 4 hours or overnight. Stir occasionally if it is convenient.

Melt the butter in a flameproof casserole and fry the prepared vegetables over a moderate heat for 2–3 minutes. Drain the meat from the marinade and add to the vegetables, stirring to blend well. Add the flour, stir well and cook for 1 minute. Gradually pour on the cider and bring to the boil, stirring. Season well, cover and cook at 180°C (350°F)/Gas 4, for $1\frac{1}{4}$–$1\frac{1}{2}$ hours.

Serves 4–6

Old-fashioned Lamb Stew with Onion Dumplings

Lamb stew is traditionally made with middle neck of lamb, a cut that is difficult to trim of all the fat. For this reason I usually make the casserole to the 'dumpling stage' the day before. The next day I lift off the lid of fat, reheat the dish and cook it with the dumplings and the peas for 20 minutes.

25 g (1 oz) butter	*2 tablespoons fresh chopped parsley*
1·35 kg (3 lb) middle neck of lamb, trimmed of fat	*salt and freshly-ground black pepper*
	100 g (4 oz) peas, frozen
2 medium-sized onions, peeled and sliced	
2 medium-sized carrots, peeled or scraped and sliced	For the onion dumplings:
2 small turnips, peeled and diced	*50 g (2 oz) butter*
1 tablespoon flour	*1 large onion, peeled and grated*
2 teaspoons dried thyme	*100 g (4 oz) fresh white breadcrumbs*
½ teaspoon ground coriander	*50 g (2 oz) self-raising flour*
600 ml (1 pint) white stock (see page 31)	*¼ teaspoon salt*
	freshly-ground black pepper
	1 egg, beaten

Melt the butter in a large pan and brown the meat on all sides. Remove the meat with a draining spoon and set aside to keep warm. Fry the onions for 4–5 minutes before adding the carrots and turnips. Cook for a further 3 minutes. Shake together the flour, thyme and coriander and stir into the vegetables in the pan. Continue stirring until the mixture is a pale golden brown, pour on the stock and stir until the sauce boils—a smoother sauce results if the stock is heated first. Return the meat to the pan, add the parsley and season well. Cover and simmer gently for $1\frac{1}{2}$ hours. Add the dumplings and the frozen peas and simmer for a further 20 minutes.

To make the dumplings, melt the butter in a pan and fry the grated onion over a moderate heat for 3–4 minutes. It should soften without colouring. Mix together the breadcrumbs, flour, salt and pepper. Pour in the onion and butter and bind with the beaten egg to make a soft dough. Flour your hands and shape the dough into 8 balls. Drop these on to the stew and cover the pan.

Serves 4

Lamb with Lemon Dumplings *(photograph facing page 116)*

With lemon dumplings simmered on top of the meat and cream stirred into the sauce just before serving, this is a hearty casserole—yet one that makes guests feel pampered.

25 g (1 oz) butter
1 medium-sized onion, peeled and
sliced
2 medium-sized carrots, peeled or
scraped and thinly sliced
1 medium-sized turnip, peeled and
diced
100 g (4 oz) button mushrooms,
wiped and halved
450 g (1 lb) lean shoulder of lamb,
trimmed and cut into 2·5-cm
(1-in) cubes
25 g (1 oz) flour
150 ml (¼ pint) white stock (see
page 31)

300 ml (½ pint) dry cider
1 teaspoon dried marjoram
salt and freshly-ground black pepper
2 tablespoons single cream
fresh chopped parsley to garnish

For the lemon dumplings:
100 g (4 oz) self-raising flour
50 g (2 oz) shredded suet
salt and freshly-ground black pepper
1 tablespoon fresh chopped parsley
grated rind and strained juice of 1
lemon
little water to mix

Melt the butter in a large flameproof casserole, add the prepared onion, carrot and turnip and cook over a moderate heat for 3–4 minutes. Add the mushrooms and lamb and cook for 3 minutes, stirring to brown the meat evenly. Shake in the flour, cook for a further minute, then gradually pour on the stock—preferably hot—and the cider, stirring until the sauce boils and thickens. Add the dried herb and season well with salt and pepper. Reduce the heat, cover and simmer for 40 minutes before adding the dumplings.

To make the dumplings, mix the flour, suet, pepper, salt and parsley together in a bowl, add the lemon rind and juice and mix with a little water to form a soft dough. Flour your hands and shape the dumplings into 8 balls. Place them on top of the casserole, cover, and continue to simmer for a further 20 minutes until the dumplings rise to the top again and are light and fluffy.

Just before serving, stir in the cream and garnish with parsley.

Serves 4

Hot Spiced Lamb

A half-hour skillet recipe, this one, with the minimum amount of preparation and fuss, yet an interesting end product.

1 tablespoon olive oil
1 medium-sized onion, peeled and
chopped
450 g (1 lb) neck fillet of lamb,
trimmed and cut into 2·5-cm
(1-in) cubes
1 tablespoon flour
1 tablespoon tomato purée
300 ml (½ pint) chicken stock (see
page 24)

1 large courgette, trimmed and
sliced
1 canned pimento, drained and
chopped
1 teaspoon paprika pepper
1 tablespoon red wine vinegar
½ teaspoon salt
freshly-ground black pepper
8 Spanish stuffed olives, sliced

Heat the oil in a frying pan and fry the onion and lamb, stirring to brown the meat evenly. Shake on the flour and stir to blend. Stir the tomato purée into the stock and gradually pour into the pan, stirring until the sauce boils and thickens—this is easier if the stock is heated first. Add the courgette, pimento, paprika pepper, vinegar, salt and pepper, stir well, cover and simmer over a low heat for 25 minutes. Scatter with sliced olives to garnish. Serve with plain boiled rice or buttered noodles.

Serves 4

Pasta Hot-pot

You can leave the casserole to simmer at a low heat while you are away from the house and add the pasta shells just before serving this not-quite-traditional meal in a pot.

3 tablespoons olive oil
900 g (2 lb) middle neck of lamb,
trimmed and cut into small pieces
2 medium-sized onions, peeled and
sliced
1 stalk celery, washed and chopped
1 tablespoon flour
salt and freshly-ground black pepper
600 ml (1 pint) white stock (see
page 31)

150 ml (¼ pint) orange juice
3 teaspoons redcurrant jelly
1 bouquet garni
100 g (4 oz) wholemeal pasta shells
or wagon wheels

For the beurre manié (optional):
15 g (½ oz) butter
15 g (½ oz) flour

Heat the oil in a 1·8-litre (3-pint) flameproof casserole and brown the lamb on all sides. Remove with a draining spoon and keep warm. Add the onion to the pan, fry over a medium heat for 4–5 minutes, add the celery and continue frying for 2 minutes. Sprinkle on the flour and cook, stirring, for 1 minute. Season well, then gradually pour on the stock and orange juice, stirring. Bring to the boil and simmer until the sauce begins to thicken. Return the lamb to the casserole and stir in the redcurrant jelly. Add the bouquet garni, cover the casserole and cook at 150°C (300°F)/Gas 2, for 2½ hours. Add the pasta shapes to the casserole and continue cooking for ½ hour or until just tender. If you like the sauce a little thicker, stir in a beurre manié of blended butter and flour. Remove the bouquet garni before serving.

Serves 4–6

Kidneys in Ale

This is the kind of dish that can be made in moments in an electric cook pan. The kidneys and the rich brown sauce cook in about the time it takes to boil the rice and you have a meal in just a quarter of an hour.

50 g (2 oz) butter
12 lambs' kidneys, skinned, halved and with the core removed
1 large onion, peeled and chopped
100 g (4 oz) streaky bacon, without rind, chopped
100 g (4 oz) button mushrooms, wiped and sliced

15 g (½ oz) flour
salt and freshly-ground black pepper
300 ml (½ pint) brown ale
1 tablespoon tomato purée
2 150-ml (5-oz) cartons fresh soured cream
parsley sprigs to garnish

Melt half the butter in a pan and cook the kidneys over a low heat for 5 minutes, stirring at intervals. Remove the kidneys with a draining spoon and set aside to keep warm. Add remaining butter to that in the pan and when it has melted cook the onion, bacon and mushrooms over a moderate heat for 5 minutes. Stir in the flour seasoned with salt and pepper, and pour on the brown ale. Stir to blend thoroughly and bring to the boil, still stirring. Add the tomato purée and boil rapidly to reduce the sauce. Return the kidneys to the pan and stir in one full carton of soured cream and one-third of the other. Reheat gently without allowing to boil. Taste, and adjust seasoning if necessary. Top with the remaining soured cream and serve with plain boiled rice. Garnish with sprigs of parsley.

Serves 4

Sherried Kidneys

From brown ale, in the previous recipe, to sherry—a little drop of something gives a dish of kidneys hidden flavour. This one is garnished with stuffed olives, bright rings of red and green.

2 tablespoons flour
large pinch of nutmeg
¼ teaspoon salt
freshly-ground black pepper
8 lambs' kidneys, skinned, halved
   and with the core removed
1 tablespoon cooking oil

150 ml (¼ pint) brown bone stock
   (see page 22)
4 tablespoons medium sherry
65 ml (2½ oz) single cream
12 stuffed green olives, halved
fresh chopped parsley to garnish

Shake together the flour, nutmeg, salt and pepper in a polythene or greaseproof paper bag and toss the kidneys in it. Heat the oil in a frying pan, shake in the kidneys and all the flour and stir well. Add the stock—hot stock will blend more easily—and sherry and stir until blended and the sauce boils, then stir in the cream and olives. Reheat without boiling and serve with buttered noodles.

Serves 4

Pork and Fruit Casserole

Sparerib chops have a good flavour—even more so when they are spiced with cinnamon and fruit.

3 tablespoons cooking oil
1 medium-sized onion, peeled and
   sliced
40 g (1½ oz) flour
salt and freshly-ground black pepper
1 teaspoon ground cinnamon
4 pork sparerib chops, trimmed of
   excess fat

300 ml (½ pint) chicken stock (see
   page 24)
300 ml (½ pint) light ale
75 g (3 oz) prunes and 75 g (3 oz)
   dried apricots, soaked overnight in
   cold tea
225 g (8 oz) potatoes, peeled and
   cut into wedges

Heat the oil in a flameproof casserole and fry the onion until beginning to turn golden brown. Toss the flour, salt, pepper and cinnamon together in a polythene or greaseproof paper bag and shake the chops in it to cover them completely. Fry the chops in the casserole, turning to brown them on both sides. Remove the meat and set aside to keep warm. Shake in any remaining seasoned flour, stir well and cook over a moderate heat for 1 minute. Gradually pour in the stock and beer, stirring until the sauce boils and thickens. (The sauce will blend better if the stock is heated first.) Drain and stone the prunes and add them with the apricots. Return the chops to the casserole, add the potato wedges, cover and cook at 180°C (350°F)/Gas 4, for 1½ hours.

Serves 4

Mr Cox's Casserole

Just as apple sauce is rightly a favourite accompaniment to roast pork, so are dessert apples a perfect ingredient in pork casseroles. Here, with fresh pear and apple jelly too, the pork basks in the fruits of a golden harvest.

40 g (1½ oz) flour
pinch of nutmeg
salt and freshly-ground black pepper
900 g (2 lb) sparerib of pork,
  trimmed of excess fat and cut into
  2·5-cm (1-in) cubes
50 g (2 oz) butter
1 onion, peeled and sliced
175 g (6 oz) button mushrooms,
  wiped and halved

450 ml (¾ pint) chicken stock (see
  page 24)
2 Cox's orange pippin apples,
  peeled, cored and sliced
1 large cooking pear, peeled, cored
  and sliced
1 tablespoon apple jelly
1 150-ml (5-oz) carton fresh soured
  cream

Shake the flour, nutmeg, salt and pepper together in a polythene or greaseproof paper bag and toss the cubes of meat in it. Melt the butter in a flameproof casserole and fry the onion for 2–3 minutes over a medium heat. Add the pork cubes and fry, stirring, until they are evenly brown. Remove from the heat, add the mushrooms and shake in any remaining seasoned flour. Gradually pour on the stock—it will blend better if it is hot—return the pan to the heat and stir until the sauce boils and thickens. Cover the casserole and cook at 180°C (350°F)/Gas 4, for 1½ hours before adding the fruit (or, for slow cooking, add it after thickening the sauce). Add the slices of apple and pear, stir in the apple jelly, cover and cook for a further 20 minutes. Stir in the soured cream and reheat without boiling.

Serves 4–6

Pork and Sage Pot *(photographed on the jacket)*

Mustard, light white wine and apples give cubes of pork a smooth spicy sauce.

3 tablespoons flour
2 tablespoons mustard powder
salt and freshly-ground black pepper
900 g (2 lb) blade or shoulder of
  pork, trimmed and cut into 2·5-cm
  (1-in) cubes
50 g (2 oz) butter
2 tablespoons cooking oil
2 medium-sized onions, peeled and
  thinly sliced

1 teaspoon dried thyme
1 teaspoon dried sage
300 ml (½ pint) white stock (see
  page 31)
300 ml (½ pint) German white wine
450 g (1 lb) dessert apples, cored
  and thickly sliced
sprigs of whole sage, if available, to
  garnish

Put the flour, mustard powder, salt and pepper into a polythene or greaseproof paper bag and toss the meat cubes in it. Heat the butter and oil together in a flameproof casserole and fry the onions until golden brown. Add the meat and stir to brown on all sides. Stir in any remaining flour and the herbs. Pour on the stock—preferably hot—and the wine, stirring until the sauce thickens and boils. Cover the casserole and cook at 180°C (350°F)/ Gas 4, for 1¼ hours. Add the apples and cook for a further 20 minutes, until they are barely soft. Decorate the dish with whole sage sprigs if available, and serve with boiled new potatoes. For a more special dish, substitute 4 whole apples and cook for the last 35–40 minutes.

Serves 4

Baker's Porkpot

I love recipes that include sausages because I consider them vastly under-rated as an ingredient. Here they accompany pork sparerib, all hot and mustardy.

550 g (1¼ lb) sparerib of pork, trimmed and cut into 2·5-cm (1-in) cubes
225 g (8 oz) large pork sausages
1 medium-sized onion, peeled and chopped
3 medium-sized carrots, peeled or scraped and sliced
3 stalks celery, washed and sliced
1 tablespoon flour

600 ml (1 pint) chicken stock (see page 24)
½ teaspoon dried rosemary, crushed
1 teaspoon soy sauce
salt and freshly-ground black pepper

For the topping:
8 1-cm (½-in) thick slices from a French loaf
French mustard

In a non-stick flameproof casserole, gently fry the pork cubes and sausages, without any additional fat. Remove the meat and cut the sausages into 2·5-cm (1-in) slices. Set aside to keep warm. Fry the prepared vegetables together in the fat that will now be in the casserole, stir in the flour and gradually pour on the stock—preferably hot. Stir until the sauce boils and thickens. Add the crushed rosemary and soy sauce and season well with salt and pepper. Return the meat to the casserole, cover and cook at 180°C (350°F)/Gas 4, for 45 minutes before adding the mustard topping.

To prepare the topping, spread the bread slices generously with mustard and place them in a ring on top of the casserole. Continue to cook, uncovered, for a further 45 minutes.

Serves 4

Pork à la Provençale

Here's a special dinner party dish in which the pot of pork is enriched with an anchovy paste towards the end of the cooking time. It's one your guests will never forget.

1·35 kg (3 lb) sparerib of pork, trimmed of excess fat and cut into 2·5-cm (1-in) cubes

For the marinade:
300 ml (½ pint) dry white wine
2 tablespoons olive oil
2 teaspoons salt
freshly-ground black pepper
½ teaspoon dried sage
½ teaspoon dried thyme
1 bayleaf, crushed
2 cloves garlic, peeled and crushed
1 large onion, peeled and thinly sliced
1 large carrot, peeled or scraped and sliced

225 g (8 oz) streaky bacon, without rind, cut into strips
100 g (4 oz) mushrooms, wiped and sliced
450 g (1 lb) tomatoes, skinned and sliced
50 g (2 oz) flour
450 ml (¾ pint) brown bone stock (see page 22)

For the anchovy paste:
10 anchovy fillets
3 tablespoons oil from anchovies (use extra olive oil to make up quantity if needed)
2 tablespoons capers
2 tablespoons red wine vinegar
2 cloves garlic, peeled and crushed
1 tablespoon fresh chopped parsley

Place the pork in a shallow dish and cover it with the marinade ingredients, mixed together. Leave in a cold place for at least 6 hours, turning the meat occasionally. Strain the marinade, reserving the liquor. Separate the meat from the marinade vegetables.

Put a few pieces of the bacon in the bottom of a large flameproof casserole and cover with a layer of the reserved marinade vegetables, then the mushrooms and tomatoes. Toss the pork in the flour and place a layer of meat over the vegetables. Continue making the layers, ending with pork and then a scattering of bacon. Pour on the reserved marinade liquor and the stock and bring to the boil. Cover the casserole and cook at 170°C (325°F)/Gas 3, for 2½ hours before adding the anchovy paste.

To make the paste, mash the anchovy fillets in the olive oil. Mash the capers into this mixture, then stir in the wine vinegar, crushed garlic and chopped parsley. Beat to a smooth paste.

Remove the casserole from the oven and skim off any fat that has risen to the top. Stir in the anchovy paste, cover, and continue cooking for 1 hour. Serve with plain boiled rice.

Serves 6

Pork with Oatmeal Cobbler

Oatmeal sprinkled over the scone topping gives a dry nuttiness which balances well with the richness of the pork.

25 g (1 oz) pork dripping or bacon fat
350 g (12 oz) belly of pork, without rind, thinly sliced
350 g (12 oz) pigs' liver, thinly sliced
1 large onion, peeled and sliced
2 medium-sized carrots, peeled or scraped and chopped
3 stalks celery, washed and sliced
25 g (1 oz) flour
450 ml (¾ pint) chicken stock (see page 24)
salt and freshly-ground black pepper
6 large sprigs of fresh sage and 1 to garnish

For the oatmeal topping:
225 g (8 oz) flour
2 teaspoons baking powder
1 teaspoon celery salt
freshly-ground black pepper
50 g (2 oz) butter
5 tablespoons milk
little extra milk to glaze
1 tablespoon medium oatmeal

Melt dripping or bacon fat in a large flameproof casserole and fry the slices of pork, stirring so that they brown evenly. Remove the meat and set aside to keep warm. Add the liver slices and fry for 2 minutes on each side to seal. Remove the liver and keep warm while you fry the prepared vegetables in the remaining fat for about 6 minutes. Sprinkle on the flour, stir well and gradually pour on the stock—preferably hot—stirring until the sauce boils and thickens. Season well with salt and pepper, return the pork and liver to the casserole and add the sprigs of sage. Cover and cook at 180°C (350°F)/Gas 4, for 1 hour before adding the scone topping.

To make the topping, sift the flour, baking powder, celery salt and pepper together in a bowl and rub in the butter. Stir in the milk to make a soft dough. On a lightly-floured board, roll out the dough to a circle large enough to fit on top of the casserole. With a sharp knife, score the top of the dough into 4 quarter sections. Increase the oven temperature to 200°C (400°F)/Gas 6.

Remove the casserole from the oven and taste for seasoning, adding more if necessary. Place the scone round on top of the meat and brush it with milk to glaze. Sprinkle the oatmeal evenly on top and cook for a further ½ hour until the topping is well risen and golden brown.

Serves 4

Glazed Pork Fillet

Packed tightly with fruit and nuts, this is an attractive one-pot way of cooking pork for a party.

2 pork fillets (sometimes called
tenderloins)
12 large prunes, soaked overnight in
water
12 whole blanched almonds

salt and freshly-ground black pepper
3 bacon rashers, without rind
3 tablespoons clear honey
150 ml (¼ pint) dry cider

Trim any excess fat from the fillets and remove the 'silver thread' which runs lengthwise along the meat. Slit down the length of each fillet and open them out flat. Stone the prunes and fill each one with a whole almond. Place a row of prunes along one fillet, season with salt and pepper and place the other fillet on top. Tie the 2 fillets firmly together with string and place in a roasting pan which has a cover. Cut the bacon rashers into strips and criss-cross them over the fillets. Spoon 2 tablespoons of honey over the top and pour on the cider. Cover the pan and roast at 190°C (375°F)/Gas 5, for 1 hour, basting occasionally with the pan juices. Ten minutes before the end of the cooking time, remove the lid and add the remaining spoonful of honey. Return the uncovered pan to the oven to glaze. Serve with plain boiled rice scattered with a few raisins.

Serves 6

Bacon Hot-pot

All orange and creamy coloured, this is a light yet filling casserole for a family meal.

675 g (1½ lb) unsmoked bacon collar
or slipper joint
40 g (1½ oz) butter
1 small onion, peeled and chopped
4 medium-sized leeks, trimmed,
washed and chopped
40 g (1½ oz) flour
450 ml (¾ pint) chicken stock (see
page 24)

2 medium-sized carrots, peeled or
scraped and sliced
225 g (8 oz) butter beans, soaked
and cooked in boiling water for 1
hour (see page 42)
1 tablespoon fresh chopped parsley
freshly-ground black pepper
550 g (1¼ lb) potatoes, peeled and
sliced

Remove the rind and any excess fat from the bacon and cut the meat into 2·5-cm (1-in) cubes. Melt the butter in a flameproof casserole, add the onion and leeks and cook over a gentle heat until they are soft but not brown. Stir in the flour, then gradually pour in the stock—preferably hot—stirring until the sauce thickens. Cook for 1 minute, then add the bacon, carrots, butter beans and parsley and season with pepper. Arrange the potato slices in rings over the top of the casserole, cover and cook at 180°C (350°F)/Gas 4, for 1½ hours. Remove the lid for the last ½ hour of the cooking time to brown the potatoes.

Serves 4

Spanish Rice

The famous Spanish paella, made with lobster, chicken, ham and so on can by no means be an everyday dish. But less costly ingredients, especially if you can buy the spicy Spanish chorizo sausage, can be turned into a delicious substitute.

4 tablespoons olive oil
100 g (4 oz) belly of pork, without rind, cut into small cubes
1 large onion, peeled and sliced
2 large cloves garlic, peeled and finely chopped
225 g (8 oz) chorizo sausage, skinned and sliced
2 canned pimentos, drained and sliced
4 large tomatoes, skinned and sliced

225 g (8 oz) unpolished rice
1 small jar mussels, drained and rinsed
25 g (1 oz) blanched almonds, slivered
600 ml (1 pint) chicken stock, boiling (see page 24)
100 g (4 oz) peas, cooked
1 tablespoon fresh chopped parsley to garnish

Heat the oil in a large, heavy pan, add the pork and fry over a high heat until the fat runs. Add the onion, garlic and sausage and fry over medium heat for 4–5 minutes until the onion is soft but not browning. Add the pimentos and tomato, stir well, and cook for 2–3 minutes before adding the rice, mussels, almonds and chicken stock. Cook over a low heat until the rice is tender and has absorbed the stock—about 40 minutes. Stir in the peas and heat through.

A paella pan is, of course, traditional for this dish which is served in the pan in which it was cooked. If you have a good-looking frying pan, don't be shy. Give the rice a final stir with a fork, sprinkle it with the parsley and bring it to the table. Otherwise, pile on to a shallow, heated serving dish.

Serves 4–6

New Orleans Jambalaya

All the ingredients in this one-pot classic are mild enough—until you come to the hot pepper sauce. That's what binds the flavours together.

50 g (2 oz) butter
2 medium-sized onions, peeled and
 chopped
1 clove garlic, peeled and finely
 chopped
1 green pepper, trimmed and
 chopped
350 g (12 oz) potatoes, peeled and
 diced
175 g (6 oz) long-grain rice
225 g (8 oz) frankfurters, halved

175 g (6 oz) ham, diced
100 g (4 oz) frozen prawns, thawed
600 ml (1 pint) chicken stock (see
 page 24)
1 bayleaf
½ teaspoon dried thyme or 1
 teaspoon fresh chopped herb
1 teaspoon red pepper sauce
salt and freshly-ground black pepper
1 tablespoon fresh chopped parsley
 to garnish

Melt the butter in a large flameproof casserole, add the onion, garlic and pepper and fry over a medium heat until onions are transparent but not brown. Add the potatoes and rice and stir quickly to coat with butter, then stir in the frankfurters, ham, prawns and chicken stock. Add the bayleaf, thyme and pepper sauce, and season with salt and black pepper. Bring to the boil, stirring, turn down the heat and simmer for 30–35 minutes until the rice and potatoes are tender and all the stock has been absorbed. (An asbestos mat under the pan will stop the dish drying out too quickly.) Remove bayleaf, stir the rice well and sprinkle with parsley.

Serves 4–6

BEEF AND VEAL

People who were brought up in a meat-and-two-veg family must find it hard to realise that our traditional way of cooking and serving meat is one of the costliest in the world. As if that alone weren't enough to make one look for other ways of cooking meat—think of the washing up! Remembering toppling mountains of pots and pans in the kitchen on a Sunday afternoon is incentive enough to pop the meat and two or more veg into a casserole, switch on and leave it to cook.

We tend to think of beef casseroles as rich, warming, winter stews, and veal dishes as lighter, more summery, and suitable for parties. There are recipes here that prove both of these assumptions right. And wrong. For beef can be cooked in golden honey, in a light stock, with sweetcorn or with beansprouts, just as well as in the dark-brown ways, with beer, bone stock, prunes and root vegetables, that are more familiar.

Veal is sometimes the subject of controversy these days, but this is not the place to enter into a discussion of rearing methods. I will only say that when I buy veal I do like to know how the calf was fed; just as I always ask for free-range eggs.

Cheap cuts of veal—sold ready cut up, often, as pie veal—are ideal for the long, slow cooking methods here. I would buy fillet of veal for casserole cooking only when—and it does happen to all of us sometimes—time was more precious than money. The veal dishes with mustard and with anchovies have the kind of 'bite' that is welcome for winter fare.

Many of the recipes in this chapter can be split into two stages. First the basic casserole of meat and vegetables prepared and partly cooked. Then if it suits your timetable best, the dish can be covered and put in a refrigerator or kept in a cold place overnight, or frozen. It is a well-known fact that practically all casserole dishes benefit from being left to stand. Each ingredient either absorbs or imparts flavour, until the harmony is smoother and more complete. Some dishes would simply need reheating, or thawing and heating. But others have a second-stage operation to perform—a scone topping, dumplings, rounds of spicy bread or a sprinkling of cheesy crumbs to complete the meal. Mix these toppings turn-and-turn-about with the basic casserole ingredients and you will be able to ring the changes endlessly.

94

Veal Seville *(photograph facing page 117)*

Escallopes of veal served with a vegetable stuffing and piquant sauce make the most of a luxury cut of meat.

100 g (4 oz) butter	*4 veal escallopes, beaten flat*
1 medium-sized onion, chopped	*25 g (1 oz) flour*
100 g (4 oz) mushrooms, wiped and	*150 ml (¼ pint) chicken stock (see*
chopped	*page 24)*
50 g (2 oz) Spanish stuffed green	*thinly-pared rind and strained juice*
olives	*of 1 orange*
50 g (2 oz) fresh white breadcrumbs	*1 tablespoon dry sherry*
1 egg, beaten	*150 ml (¼ pint) single cream*
salt and freshly-ground black pepper	

Melt half the butter in a pan and fry the onion over a moderate heat for 4–5 minutes. Add the mushrooms and cook for 2 more minutes, then remove the pan from the heat. Chop half the olives and add them to the pan with the breadcrumbs. Stir well, bind with the beaten egg, and season with salt and pepper. Place the escallopes on a chopping board and spread each one with the stuffing mixture. Roll up the escallopes and tie with string or secure with cocktail sticks. Melt the remaining butter in the same pan and fry the rolls, turning them frequently to brown them on all sides. Remove the cooked rolls to a warm serving dish and keep hot while you make the sauce. Stir the flour in the pan and gradually pour in the stock—preferably hot—stirring until the sauce thickens. Add the strained juice of the orange, the sherry and cream and heat without boiling. Pour the sauce over the veal rolls and garnish with thin strips of orange rind and the remaining olives, halved.

Serves 4

Mustard Veal

Cream and mustard combine to make a smooth, slightly spicy sauce in which to cook the veal.

2 tablespoons cooking oil	*just over 300 ml (½ pint) chicken*
900 g (2 lb) pie veal, trimmed and	*stock or white stock (see pages 24*
cut into 2·5-cm (1-in) cubes	*and 31)*
225-g (8-oz) piece of bacon,	*salt and freshly-ground black pepper*
without rind, cut into 2·5-cm	*1 bouquet garni*
(1-in) cubes	*150 ml (¼ pint) double cream*
2 medium-sized onions, peeled and	*2 tablespoons Dijon mustard*
sliced	*1 tablespoon fresh chopped parsley*
1 tablespoon flour	

Heat the oil in a flameproof casserole and add the veal, stirring to brown it evenly. Remove the veal and set aside to keep warm. Add the bacon to the oil in the pan and fry over a moderate heat for 5–6 minutes until the fat runs. Add the onion and fry for 2–3 minutes, then stir in the flour and gradually pour on the stock, stirring until the sauce thickens—it will be smoother if you heat the stock first. Return the veal to the casserole, add seasoning, cover and cook at 180°C (350°F)/Gas 4, for 1½–2 hours, until the meat is tender. Stir in a little more hot stock during this time if needed.

Remove the bouquet garni and stir in the cream, mustard and parsley. Return to the oven for a few minutes to reheat the sauce before serving.

Serves 4–6

Summer Veal

Few butchers where I live stock veal, so I light upon even the humblest cuts as a rarity, to be sought after when I go into town. This casserole is green and creamy, slow-cooked in a white wine sauce.

2 tablespoons cooking oil
25 g (1 oz) butter
2 medium-sized onions, peeled and finely sliced
1 clove garlic, peeled and finely chopped
2 tablespoons flour
salt and freshly-ground black pepper
¼ teaspoon turmeric
½ teaspoon dried dill leaves

675 g (1½ lb) pie veal, trimmed and cut into 2·5-cm (1-in) cubes
100 g (4 oz) mushrooms, wiped and sliced
2 medium-sized carrots, peeled or scraped and sliced
3 stalks celery, washed and sliced
1 green pepper, trimmed and cut into strips
150 ml (¼ pint) dry white wine
1 tablespoon fresh chopped parsley

Heat the oil and butter together in a flameproof casserole and sauté the onion and garlic over a moderate heat for 3–4 minutes. Shake the flour, salt, pepper, turmeric and dill together in a polythene or greaseproof paper bag and toss the meat cubes, a few at a time, to coat them with the seasoned flour. Add the veal to the casserole and stir well before adding the prepared vegetables and any remaining flour. Stir in the wine and parsley, cover and cook at 170°C (325°F)/Gas 3, for 1 hour, stirring once or twice. Serve with plain boiled rice.

Serves 4

Veal with Tarragon

Lemon and tarragon, often associated with chicken dishes, are refreshing flavours with veal, too.

50 g (2 oz) butter
900 g (2 lb) pie veal, trimmed and
  cut into 2.5-cm (1-in) cubes
1 medium-sized onion, peeled and
  sliced
1 tablespoon flour
150 ml (¼ pint) chicken stock (see
  page 24)
150 ml (¼ pint) dry cider
salt and freshly-ground black pepper

1½ teaspoons dried tarragon (or
  marjoram)
grated rind and juice of 1 lemon
100 g (4 oz) mushrooms, wiped and
  sliced
150-ml (¼-pint) carton fresh soured
  cream
2 egg yolks
1 tablespoon fresh chopped parsley
lemon slices to garnish

Melt the butter in a flameproof casserole and brown the meat cubes a few at a time. Remove each batch with a draining spoon and set aside to keep warm. Fry the onion in the casserole and when it is soft sprinkle on the flour and stir to take up the juices. Pour on the stock, stirring to form a thick sauce—this will be easier if the stock is hot—then add the cider, still stirring. Add the seasoning, the dried herb, lemon rind and the mushrooms, stir well, then return the meat to the casserole. Cover and cook at 150°C (300°F)/Gas 2, for 2½ hours. Blend the soured cream and egg yolks together and stir into the sauce. Add the lemon juice, then return the casserole to the oven to heat. Sprinkle with parsley and decorate with lemon slices. Serve with plain boiled rice.

Serves 4–6

Anchovy Veal and Ham

Fillet of veal is used for this party dish. If you prefer to substitute another cut of meat, increase both the marinating and the cooking time so that the meat emerges just as tender.

450 g (1 lb) fillet of veal, trimmed
  and cut into strips
225 g (8 oz) ham, trimmed and cut
  into 1-cm (½-in) cubes
300 ml (½ pint) dry cider
few peppercorns
1 bayleaf
50 g (2 oz) butter
100 g (4 oz) mushrooms, sliced

2 medium-sized carrots, peeled or
  scraped and thinly sliced
50 g (2 oz) anchovy fillets, rinsed,
  dried and halved
½ teaspoon dried oregano
2 150-ml (¼-pint) cartons fresh
  soured cream
croûtons to garnish (see page 37)

Put the veal and ham together in a bowl and pour on the cider. Add the peppercorns and bayleaf and leave to marinate for 1½–2 hours, turning the meats over once or twice. Drain, discard the peppercorns and bayleaf and reserve the liquor.

Melt the butter in a flameproof casserole and fry the meat, stirring to brown the pieces evenly on all sides. Pour on the reserved marinade and add the prepared vegetables, the anchovies and the herb. Stir well, cover the casserole and cook at 150°C (300°F)/Gas 2, for ½ hour. Stir in the soured cream, reserving a little to garnish. Return the casserole to the oven, without the lid, and reheat. Spoon the reserved soured cream over and garnish with croûtons before serving.

Serves 4

Beef and Watercress Rolls

A variation of beef olives, given an extra 'bite' with chopped watercress in the filling.

100 g (4 oz) fresh brown breadcrumbs	*8 thin slices blade bone of beef, beaten flat*
1 spring onion, trimmed and finely chopped	*50 g (2 oz) butter*
grated rind and strained juice of 1 lemon	*450 g (1 lb) courgettes, sliced*
	450 ml (¾ pint) chicken or white stock (see pages 24 and 31)
450 g (1 lb) large tomatoes, skinned and mashed	*1 bayleaf*
2 bunches watercress, washed and chopped (but reserve a few sprigs to garnish)	*salt and freshly-ground black pepper*
	450 g (1 lb) new potatoes, scraped and quartered

In a bowl, mix together the breadcrumbs, onion, lemon rind and juice and 2 of the tomatoes, and stir in the watercress. Divide the mixture between the 8 pieces of beef. Spread it evenly over them and roll up, securing with string or cocktail sticks. Melt the butter in a flameproof casserole and brown the meat rolls evenly on all sides. Remove and set aside to keep warm. Add the courgettes, stir well, then add the remaining tomatoes, the stock and bayleaf, and season well. Bring the sauce to the boil, return the meat rolls and turn them in the sauce to cover them. Cover the casserole and cook at 180°C (350°F)/Gas 4, for ¾ hour before adding the potato. Cook for a further ½ hour, removing the lid for the last 15 minutes of the cooking time. Remove the bayleaf, and garnish with the reserved watercress sprigs.

Serves 4

Beef and Noodle Casserole

Noodles cooked with the meat, and cheese stirred in just before serving make this a filling and complete one-pot dish.

3 tablespoons cooking oil
1 medium-sized onion, peeled and
  chopped
2 cloves garlic, peeled and crushed
2 green peppers, trimmed and sliced
2 stalks celery, washed and sliced
450 g (1 lb) minced beef
1 350-g (12-oz) can beansprouts,
  drained

1 tablespoon fresh chopped parsley
1 400-g (15-oz) can tomatoes
300 ml ($\frac{1}{2}$ pint) chicken stock (see
  page 24)
75 g (3 oz) black olives, stoned and
  halved
225 g (8 oz) noodles, uncooked
salt and freshly-ground black pepper
100 g (4 oz) cheese, cut in small cubes

Heat the oil in a flameproof casserole and sauté the onion, garlic, pepper and celery for 4–5 minutes over a moderate heat until beginning to turn golden brown. Add the minced beef and stir so that it browns evenly. Add the remaining ingredients, except the cheese, and stir well. Cover the casserole and cook at 170°C (325°F)/Gas 3, for 1$\frac{1}{4}$ hours, stirring once or twice during the cooking time. Add the cheese cubes and return the casserole, uncovered, to the oven for about 10 minutes, until the cheese begins to melt.

Serves 4

Beef Cobbler

The meat mixture is first browned and simmered in a casserole, then a high-rise cheese scone topping is arranged over it.

25 g (1 oz) butter
1 large onion, peeled and chopped
1 clove garlic, peeled and finely
  chopped
450 g (1 lb) minced beef
100 g (4 oz) mushrooms, wiped and
  chopped
50 g (2 oz) flour
1 400-g (15-oz) can tomatoes
1 tablespoon tomato purée
1 teaspoon mixed dried herbs

pinch of sugar
pinch of grated nutmeg
salt and freshly-ground black pepper

For the topping:
225 g (8 oz) self-raising flour
$\frac{1}{4}$ teaspoon salt
50 g (2 oz) margarine
150 ml ($\frac{1}{4}$ pint) milk
75 g (3 oz) cheese, grated
egg or milk to glaze

Melt the butter in a 1·2-litre (2-pint) flameproof casserole and sauté the onion and garlic for 3–4 minutes over a moderate heat, then add the minced beef and stir to brown it evenly. Add the mushrooms and sprinkle on the flour. Stir well and remove from the heat. Pour on the can of tomatoes and add the tomato purée, herbs, sugar and nutmeg and season well with salt and pepper. Return the casserole to a low heat and bring it slowly to the boil, stirring to prevent the mixture from sticking. Cook gently for 10 minutes while you make the scone topping.

Sift the flour and salt into a bowl and rub in the margarine. Stir in the milk and mix well to form a soft dough. Knead lightly on a floured board and roll to an oblong about 37 × 18 cm (15 × 7 in). Sprinkle the cheese over the dough and roll up loosely lengthwise. Cut into 12 slices, a swiss roll of dough with a cheese filling. Overlap the slices round the edge of the casserole, with one in the centre, and brush with beaten egg or milk to glaze. Stand the casserole on a baking sheet and bake at 200°C (400°F)/Gas 6, for 30–35 minutes, until the scone topping is well risen and golden brown.

Serves 4

Beef with Horseradish Dumplings

Your favourite beef casserole—this one is a fairly standard recipe—is tremendously enriched by the addition of horseradish dumplings, 20 minutes before the end of the cooking time.

25 g (1 oz) flour
salt and freshly-ground black pepper
pinch of ground allspice
½ teaspoon dried thyme
675 g (1½ lb) stewing steak,
* trimmed and cut into 2·5-cm*
* (1-in) cubes*
40 g (1½ oz) butter
2 medium-sized onions, peeled and
* sliced*
2 stalks celery, washed and sliced

600 ml (1 pint) brown bone stock
* (see page 22)*
1 tablespoon tomato purée

For the dumplings:
100 g (4 oz) self-raising flour
1 teaspoon salt
40 g (1½ oz) shredded suet
1 tablespoon horseradish sauce
3–4 tablespoons cold water to mix

Mix the flour, salt, pepper, allspice and herb together in a polythene or greaseproof paper bag and toss the meat, a little at a time, so that it is well covered in seasoned flour. Remove it and reserve any remaining flour. Melt the butter in a large pan and fry the onion and celery until golden brown. Add the meat and fry for a further 5 minutes, stirring to brown it evenly on all sides. Stir in any remaining flour and remove the pan from the heat. Mix the stock—preferably hot—and tomato purée together and, over a medium heat, gradually pour the liquid over the meat, stirring. Bring the sauce to the boil, lower the heat and simmer, covered, for 2 hours, adding the dumplings 20 minutes before the end of the cooking time.

To make the dumplings, mix together the flour, salt and suet in a bowl. Blend the horseradish sauce and water together and add to the flour. Mix to form a soft dough. Shape the dough into 8 balls and place on top of the stew for the last 20 minutes.

Serves 4

Honey Beef Stew

Beef takes well to the golden sweetness of honey, which makes this dish lighter and less rich than most.

2 tablespoons cooking oil
675 g (1½ lb) stewing beef, trimmed and cut into 2·5-cm (1-in) cubes
1 medium-sized onion, peeled and sliced
1 green pepper, trimmed and sliced
2 medium-sized carrots, peeled or scraped and sliced

2 stalks celery, washed and sliced
2 tablespoons clear honey
juice of ½ lemon, strained
1 tablespoon tomato purée
300 ml (½ pint) brown bone stock (see page 22)
550 g (1¼ lb) new potatoes, scraped and quartered

Heat the oil in a flameproof casserole and fry the meat, stirring to brown it evenly. Add the prepared vegetables and cook for a further 5 minutes. Remove the casserole from the heat. Mix together the honey, lemon juice, tomato purée and stock and pour into the casserole. Stir well and cook at 180°C (350°F)/Gas 4, for 1½ hours, adding the potatoes for the last 40 minutes of the cooking time.

Serves 4

Beef with Cabbage

Layers of meat, cabbage and the crisp topping make a complete meal with an interesting contrast of textures, yet only one casserole dish to wash up after dinner!

25 g (1 oz) flour
salt and freshly-ground black pepper
675 g (1½ lb) stewing steak, trimmed and cut into 2·5-cm (1-in) cubes
25 g (1 oz) butter
2 medium-sized onions, peeled and sliced
1 tablespoon tomato purée
450 ml (¾ pint) brown bone stock (see page 22)
1 medium-sized carrot, peeled or scraped and sliced

½ teaspoon mixed dried herbs
1 small white cabbage, trimmed and shredded

For the topping:
40 g (1½ oz) butter
50 g (2 oz) fresh white breadcrumbs
225 g (8 oz) self-raising flour
1 teaspoon salt
freshly-ground black pepper
½ teaspoon dried onion powder
3 tablespoons cooking oil
150 ml (¼ pint) milk

Well season the flour with salt and pepper, tip into a polythene or greaseproof paper bag and shake the meat cubes until they are thoroughly coated. Melt the butter in a 1·8-litre (3-pint) flameproof casserole and fry the onion until it is golden brown. Add the meat and stir so that it browns evenly on all sides. Remove the casserole from the heat. Stir the tomato purée into the stock—preferably heated first—and pour into the casserole. Add the carrot and herbs, return to the heat and stir until the sauce boils. Cover the casserole and cook at 170°C (325°F)/Gas 3, for 1½ hours before you add the cabbage and the topping.

To make the topping, melt the butter in a pan and fry the breadcrumbs until they have absorbed all the fat and are completely dry. Sift the flour, salt, pepper and onion powder together into a bowl and pour in the oil and milk. Mix to form a soft dough. Drop tablespoons of the dough into the buttered crumbs and roll up into balls. Flatten slightly to make hamburger shapes.

When the casserole has been cooking for 1½ hours, spread the shredded cabbage over the meat, then arrange the rounds of dough on top.

Increase the oven heat to 190°C (375°F)/Gas 5, and bake for 40 minutes until the topping is crisp and golden brown.

Serves 4

Winter Beef

After long slow cooking the sauce is a rich reddish brown. Don't tell your guests until they have enjoyed the meal that this effect is achieved with a cup of strong black coffee!

3 tablespoons cooking oil	900 g (2 lb) stewing beef, trimmed
2 medium-sized onions, peeled and	and cut into fingers
sliced	50 g (2 oz) raisins
2 cloves garlic, peeled and finely	50 g (2 oz) mushrooms, wiped and
chopped	sliced
1 tablespoon flour	150 ml (¼ pint) strong black coffee
¼ teaspoon dried marjoram	350 g (12 oz) tomatoes, halved
1 teaspoon paprika	150 ml (¼ pint) red wine
salt and freshly-ground black pepper	3 tablespoons natural yoghurt

Heat the oil in a flameproof casserole and sauté the onion and garlic over a moderate heat for 3–4 minutes. Toss the flour, marjoram, paprika, salt and pepper together in a polythene or greaseproof paper bag and shake the pieces of beef until they are thoroughly coated. Add the beef to the casserole and fry, stirring to brown the meat evenly on all sides. Add the raisins, mushrooms and coffee and stir well, then add the tomatoes, cut sides down. Cover the casserole and cook at 140°C (275°F)/Gas 1, for 2½ hours. Add the wine and yoghurt, stirring carefully to avoid breaking up the tomatoes. Cover the casserole again and cook for a further ½ hour. Serve with plain boiled rice.

Serves 4–6

Beef and Potato Casserole

Potatoes cooked in the same pot with the beef absorb the flavour of the sauce until they are no longer a separate ingredient.

4 tablespoons cooking oil
675 g (1½ lb) chuck steak, trimmed
  and cut into thin strips
1 large onion, peeled and sliced
2 cloves garlic, peeled and finely
  chopped
2 stalks celery, washed and sliced
2 large tomatoes, skinned and sliced
2 tablespoons tomato purée

300 ml (½ pint) brown bone stock
  (see page 22)
2 tablespoons fresh chopped parsley
2 tablespoons celery leaves, finely
  chopped
salt and freshly-ground black pepper
675 g (1½ lb) potatoes, peeled and
  sliced

Heat the oil until smoking in a flameproof casserole and fry the pieces of beef a few at a time until they are browned on both sides. Keep the first batches warm while you fry the others. Add the onion to the oil in the casserole and fry over a moderate heat for 2–3 minutes before adding the garlic and celery. Fry for a further 3 minutes, then return the beef to the casserole and add the tomatoes, the tomato purée stirred into the stock and the parsley and celery leaves. Season well with salt and pepper and bring the sauce to the boil. This will be smoother if the stock was heated first. Cover and simmer for ¾ hour, then add the potato slices and stir to cover them thoroughly with the sauce. Continue to simmer, covered, for ½ hour, until the potatoes are tender. Serve with a crisp green vegetable such as cabbage or broccoli.

Serves 4

Carbonnade of Beef

Beer marinade tenderises and enriches the beef and the mustard topping seals in the goodness.

675 g (1½ lb) topside of beef,
  trimmed and cut into large strips
300 ml (½ pint) brown ale
150 ml (¼ pint) brown bone stock
  (see page 22)
350 g (12 oz) shallots, peeled
2 medium-sized carrots, peeled or
  scraped and sliced
1 bouquet garni

50 g (2 oz) butter
40 g (1½ oz) flour
salt and freshly-ground black pepper
1 dessertspoon soft dark brown sugar
1 teaspoon French mustard

For the topping:
slices of French bread
French mustard

Put the beef in a shallow dish with the ale, stock, prepared vegetables and the bouquet garni and leave to marinate overnight.

Next day, melt the butter in a flameproof casserole. Toss the meat in flour well seasoned with salt and pepper and fry it a few pieces at a time. Remove each batch with a draining spoon and set aside to keep warm. Strain the marinade, reserving the liquor. Sauté the strained shallots in the casserole until they turn light brown, sprinkle on the remaining seasoned flour, stir well, then pour on the marinade, stirring until the sauce thickens. Stir in the sugar and mustard and return the meat to the casserole. Cover and cook at 150°C (300°F)/Gas 2, for 2 hours. You can prepare the dish to this stage, then leave overnight before adding the mustard topping and reheating.

Cover the casserole with slices of French bread spread with mustard, mustard side up, trimming the slices so that there are no gaps. Increase the oven temperature to 200°C (400°F)/Gas 6, and cook, uncovered, for a further $\frac{1}{2}$ hour. Push the bread slices down into the sauce once or twice during the cooking time.

Serves 4

Ragout of Beef

If it's a good rich casserole you're after, this is the one. It's as dark and warming as a Christmas pudding, yet undeniably still a beef stew.

2 tablespoons cooking oil	*675 g (1½ lb) stewing steak,*
100 g (4 oz) streaky bacon, without	*trimmed and cut into 2·5-cm*
rind, chopped	*(1-in) cubes*
1 medium-sized onion, peeled and	*300 ml (½ pint) brown bone stock*
sliced	*(see page 22)*
2 stalks celery, washed and chopped	*grated rind and juice of 1 orange*
25 g (1 oz) flour	*100 g (4 oz) prunes, stones*
salt and freshly-ground black pepper	*removed, soaked overnight*

Heat the oil in a flameproof casserole and sauté the bacon for 3–4 minutes over a moderate heat. Add the onion and celery and cook for a further 3–4 minutes. Toss the flour, well seasoned with salt and pepper, in a polythene or greaseproof paper bag and shake the cubes of meat to coat them well. Add the meat and any remaining flour to the casserole and stir well to blend, then gradually pour in the stock, stirring. The sauce will be easier to blend if the stock is hot. Add the orange rind and juice and the prunes, stir well and bring to the boil gradually. Cover the casserole and cook at 170°C (325°F)/Gas 3, for 2¼–2½ hours, until the meat is tender. Serve with baked jacket potatoes.

Serves 4

Beef and Onions, Greek-style

This dish is a Greek version of boeuf Bourguignonne, beef cooked with whole onions in red wine.

4 tablespoons cooking oil
675 g (1½ lb) chuck steak, trimmed
    and cut into 2·5-cm (1-in) cubes
1 large onion, peeled and sliced
2 cloves garlic, peeled and crushed
2 tablespoons tomato purée
150 ml (¼ pint) white stock (see
    page 31)

150 ml (¼ pint) dry red wine
4 tablespoons malt vinegar
1 bayleaf
salt and freshly-ground black pepper
675 g (1½ lb) small onions or
    shallots, peeled

Heat the oil until smoking in a flameproof casserole and fry the meat cubes a few at a time, stirring so that they brown evenly on all sides. Remove the cooked meat with a draining spoon and set aside to keep warm. Add the onion and garlic to the oil in the casserole and cook over a moderate heat for 4–5 minutes. Remove from the heat. Return the meat to the casserole and pour on the tomato purée stirred into the stock—preferably heated first. Add the wine, vinegar and bayleaf and season well with salt and pepper. Bring the sauce to the boil, stir well, cover the casserole and simmer for ½ hour. Add the whole onions and continue to simmer for a further 40 minutes. Remove the bayleaf. Serve with potato slices steamed over the casserole, or with whole new boiled potatoes.

Serves 4

Beef Goulash

Soured cream in the sauce and poured over the cooked dish as a garnish gives this beef casserole a decidedly Russian air. Be sparing with the paprika pepper the first time you try the recipe if you are not sure how much you like.

2 tablespoons cooking oil
3 medium-sized onions, peeled and
    sliced
1–2 tablespoons paprika pepper,
    according to taste
1 tablespoon flour
salt and freshly-ground black pepper

675 g (1¼ lb) stewing steak,
    trimmed and cut into 2·5-cm
    (1-in) cubes
1 225-g (8-oz) can tomatoes
2 150-ml (5-oz) cartons fresh
    soured cream
1 tablespoon fresh chopped parsley
    to garnish

Heat the oil in a flameproof casserole and sauté the onions over a medium heat for 4–5 minutes. Add the paprika pepper, stir well and cook for a further

2 minutes. Season the flour well with salt and pepper and toss the cubes of steak in it to cover them thoroughly. Add the meat to the casserole and fry for about 8 minutes, stirring occasionally so that the cubes brown on all sides. Tip in the tomatoes, bring the sauce to the boil, reduce the heat and simmer, covered, for 2–2¼ hours until the meat is tender. Stir in one full carton of soured cream and a third of the other one and stir well until the sauce is smooth. Reheat the casserole over a very low heat so that the sauce does not boil. Taste and add more seasoning if necessary. Pour the remaining soured cream over the meat and sprinkle with parsley to garnish. Serve with buttered noodles.

Serves 4

Beef with Sweetcorn

Some casseroles of beef have the virtue of being dark and rich. This one, with light stock and sweetcorn, would not be out of place in the heat of summer.

2 tablespoons oil	salt and freshly-ground black pepper
900 g (2 lb) chuck steak, trimmed and cut into 2·5-cm (1-in) cubes	1 bouquet garni
	175 g (6 oz) sweetcorn kernels
2 medium-sized onions, peeled and sliced	1 tablespoon chopped parsley
2 stalks celery, washed and sliced	For the topping (optional):
1 tablespoon flour	50 g (2 oz) butter
450 ml (¾ pint) white stock (see page 31)	100 g (4 oz) fresh white breadcrumbs
1 tablespoon tomato purée	25 g (1 oz) cheese, finely grated

Heat the oil in a flameproof casserole and fry the meat a few cubes at a time, stirring to brown them on all sides. Remove the meat with a draining spoon and set aside to keep warm. Sauté the onion and celery for 3–4 minutes, return the meat to the casserole and sprinkle in the flour. Mix together the stock and tomato purée and pour this liquid into the casserole gradually, stirring until the sauce thickens and boils. The sauce will blend more readily if the stock is heated first. Season well with salt and pepper and add the bouquet garni. Cover and cook at 170°C (325°F)/Gas 3, for 1½ hours, then add the corn kernels and continue cooking for ½ hour. Remove the bouquet garni and stir in the parsley. Sprinkle with the topping before serving.

To make the cheese topping, melt the butter in a frying pan and stir in the breadcrumbs. Fry over a moderate heat until the crumbs have absorbed all the fat and are dry. Stir in the cheese just before garnishing the dish.

Serves 4

Brisket in Cider

Here's a dish that couldn't be easier. Marinate the beef overnight in a casserole, add a handful of fruit the next morning and pop it into a pan, to be ready for lunch.

1·35-kg (3-lb) piece of brisket of beef
300 ml (½ pint) dry cider
4 tablespoons red wine vinegar
1 medium-sized onion, peeled and sliced

1 bayleaf
salt and freshly-ground black pepper
10–12 prunes, soaked separately overnight, stoned
2 cooking apples, peeled, cored and sliced

Put the whole piece of beef in a flameproof casserole with the cider, wine vinegar, sliced onion and bayleaf. Cover and leave overnight in the refrigerator or a cool place, turning the meat over once if it is convenient. The next day, season the marinade well with salt and pepper and add the soaked, drained prunes and sliced apple. Cover the casserole and cook at 170°C (325°F)/Gas 3, for 2 hours, until the beef is tender. Serve with mashed potatoes.

Serves 4–6

Pul Ko-Kee

This Korean dish features sirloin of beef in a more economical way than we are accustomed to serve it. And it cooks in about a quarter of an hour.

1 tablespoon olive oil
4 tablespoons caster sugar
6 tablespoons soy sauce
1 teaspoon red pepper sauce
1 clove garlic, peeled and crushed
1 tablespoon sesame seed (optional)

1 tablespoon flour
1 small onion, peeled and grated
450 g (1 lb) beef sirloin, trimmed and cut into thin strips
150 ml (¼ pint) water

Whisk together in a bowl the oil, sugar, soy sauce, pepper sauce, garlic, sesame seed if used and flour. Put onion and strips of meat into a flameproof casserole and pour on the marinade. Stir well, cover and leave to stand for ½ hour. Add the water to the marinade and bring to the boil, stirring. Cover the casserole and simmer over a low heat for 15–20 minutes until the meat is tender. Serve with plain boiled rice.

Serves 4

VEGETABLES

It often seems that there are two kinds of vegetables, those that accompany a meat or fish dish, and those that are served as a course of their own. That's not really so, because all the vegetables that usually form only part of the chorus can indeed play the lead in any meal, however formal.

With the cost of protein foods rising so rapidly throughout the world, and the fact that eventually world supplies could be inadequate to meet demand, it makes sense to develop the vegetable habit. Meatless days need not be a matter of fasting or self-denial. They can offer a varied and glorious cuisine. Add cheese to your vegetable repertoire, and you have infinite versatility.

When, because of the weather or other shortage factors, even vegetables are not exactly inexpensive, we can look for ways to make the most of a limited supply. Vegetable flans and quiches, pies and pizzas are interesting main dishes; pilaffs and risottos are always popular; and stews and hot-pots, a mixture usually of a number of vegetables, are as warm and welcoming as any meat dish.

Don't dismiss any one recipe because you don't happen to like, say, swedes or turnips; substitute potatoes or celeriac or any others you do enjoy. And never be tempted to pay exhorbitant prices for vegetables out of season. Make a note of the recipe and enjoy it all the more cheaply when its turn comes round.

Vegetable Hot-pot

Vary the vegetables in this country hot-pot according to what you have in the garden or what is cheap in the shops. Parsnips, swedes or mushrooms are all good cooked in this way.

40 g (1½ oz) butter
1 large onion, peeled and sliced
2 leeks, trimmed, washed and sliced
2 large carrots, peeled or scraped and sliced
2 medium-sized turnips, peeled and sliced
2 stalks celery, washed and chopped
40 g (1½ oz) flour

450 ml (¾ pint) chicken stock (see page 24)
2 teaspoons Worcestershire sauce
salt and freshly-ground black pepper
450 g (1 lb) potatoes, peeled and sliced
75 g (3 oz) cheese, grated
triangles of toast to serve

Melt the butter in a 1·2-litre (2-pint) flameproof casserole and fry the onion, leek, carrot, turnip and celery for 8–10 minutes, then remove the vegetables with a draining spoon. Shake the flour into the casserole and stir well to blend with the butter. Gradually pour in the chicken stock (preferably hot) and the Worcestershire sauce and bring to the boil, stirring all the time. Season well with salt and pepper and cook for 3–4 minutes until the sauce has thickened. Return the vegetables to the casserole, mix them well with the sauce and arrange the potatoes in rings on the top. Cover the casserole with the lid, stand on a baking sheet and cook at 180°C (350°F)/Gas 4, for 1½ hours, until the vegetables are tender. Remove the casserole from the oven and sprinkle the cheese over the potatoes. Increase the heat to 200°C (400°F)/Gas 6, and cook, uncovered, for 15–20 minutes until the melted cheese is golden brown.
   Serve with triangles of toast.

Serves 4

Root Vegetable Casserole

This four-in-a-pot method is an easy and economical way of cooking a selection of vegetables to accompany the meat for a dinner party—one dish on the table instead of several. But with soup first, and hot crusty bread, the casserole makes a good lunch or supper dish in its own right.

50 g (2 oz) butter
2 large onions, peeled and chopped
2 medium-sized parsnips, peeled and sliced
2 medium-sized turnips, peeled and sliced

450 g (1 lb) potatoes, peeled and sliced
salt and freshly-ground black pepper
450 ml (¾ pint) milk

Melt half the butter in a 1·2-litre (2-pint) flameproof casserole and fry the onion for 4–5 minutes, to soften. Remove the onion with a draining spoon. Brush the sides and inside lid of the casserole with the melted butter.

Sprinkle a layer of the onion in the base of the casserole and add layers of the other vegetables, adding onion and seasoning between each one. Finish with a layer of potatoes. Cut the remaining butter in small pieces and scatter on top of the dish. Pour on the milk and cover with the lid. Stand the casserole on a baking sheet and cook at 190°C (375°F)/Gas 5, for 1½ hours, removing the lid for the final ½ hour to brown the top.

Serves 4

Mediterranean Stew

This is the kind of delicious, aromatic vegetable pot that makes one say 'who needs meat?' It is at its best washed down with dry white wine.

4 tablespoons olive oil
1 large onion, peeled and sliced
2 cloves garlic, peeled and crushed
2 medium-sized aubergines, sliced
4 small courgettes, sliced slantwise
3 large tomatoes, skinned and sliced,
  or 1 small can tomatoes

4 stalks celery, washed and sliced
2 tablespoons celery leaves, washed
  and chopped
1 tablespoon fresh chopped parsley
salt and freshly-ground black pepper
1 small wineglass dry white wine

Heat the oil in a large flameproof casserole and fry the onion and garlic over a medium heat for 3–4 minutes until beginning to soften. Add the aubergine and stir well to coat with the oil, then add the remaining vegetables and the parsley. Season well with salt and pepper and pour on the wine. Cover and simmer for 45 minutes, by which time the vegetables should have completely absorbed the wine. If they have not, remove the lid and turn up the heat for the last 5 minutes.

Serve with hot garlic bread.

Serves 4

Vegetable Pot-pourri

Cooked in this way, a variety of vegetables share the same pot yet declare independence of flavours. You really can taste each one separately.

25 g (1 oz) butter
1 small cauliflower, washed and cut into florets
4 medium-sized potatoes, peeled and sliced
2 medium-sized parsnips, peeled and sliced
1 large onion, peeled and sliced
1 medium-sized leek, washed and sliced

salt and freshly-ground black pepper
100 g (4 oz) cheese, grated
2 teaspoons yeast extract
300 ml (½ pint) milk, heated

For the topping:
25 g (1 oz) fresh white breadcrumbs
50 g (2 oz) cheese, grated

Grease a 900-ml (1½-pint) flameproof casserole and arrange the prepared vegetables in layers, sprinkling cheese and seasoning between each layer with salt and pepper. Stir the yeast extract into the milk and pour over the vegetables. Cover, stand the casserole on a baking sheet and cook at 180°C (350°F)/Gas 4, for 1 hour. Sprinkle on the breadcrumbs and grated cheese, combined together, and cook, uncovered, for a further ½ hour.

Serves 4

Cauliflower in Curry Sauce

White vegetables are extremely good with a light curry sauce. Serve this one with colourful side dishes of green pepper and onion rings, tomato and poppadoms, and it's a meal in a moment.

50 g (2 oz) butter
1 small onion, peeled and sliced
1 tablespoon curry paste
juice of ½ lemon, strained
1 tablespoon cider vinegar
150 ml (¼ pint) chicken stock (see page 24)
salt

1 large cauliflower or 2 small ones, trimmed and cut into florets
1 cooking apple, peeled, cored and chopped
2 tablespoons natural yoghurt
25 g (1 oz) blanched almonds to garnish

Melt the butter in a flameproof casserole and fry the onion for 3–4 minutes over a moderate heat. Remove the casserole from the heat. Mix together the curry paste, lemon juice, cider vinegar and chicken stock and pour into the pan. Stir to blend and season with salt. Add the cauliflower to the sauce and simmer for 15–20 minutes until almost tender—this will depend on the size of the florets—then add the apple for a further 5 minutes. Stir in the yoghurt and scatter the almonds over to garnish.

Serves 4

Cauliflower with Tomato

Our appreciation of cauliflower often seems to stop short at cauliflower cheese—here the vegetable is cooked to a pinky tenderness with tomatoes, and sprinkled with cheese to serve.

40 g (1½ oz) butter
1 large onion, peeled and chopped
1 clove garlic, peeled and crushed
1 400-g (15-oz) can tomatoes
juice of ½ lemon
1 tablespoon fresh chopped parsley

½ teaspoon dried oregano
salt and freshly-ground black pepper
2 small cauliflowers, divided into
  florets
50 g (2 oz) cheese, grated, to serve

Melt the butter in a large flameproof casserole and fry the onion and garlic over a moderate heat for 4–5 minutes until transparent but not browning. Add the tomatoes with the liquor in the can, the lemon juice and herbs and season well with salt and pepper. Stir well, bring to the boil, then add the cauliflower florets. Cover the pan and simmer over a low heat for 25–30 minutes. Serve sprinkled with grated cheese.

Serves 4

Potato Feast

One summer in Greece, I promised, on the spur of the moment, to return again in the autumn. The farmworker we were staying with clapped his hands and said he would prepare a feast for our arrival, with everything on the table homegrown. He did, too. It was this.

4 tablespoons olive oil
1 large onion, peeled and chopped
1 clove garlic, peeled and crushed
900 g (2 lb) potatoes, peeled and
  sliced

4 large tomatoes, skinned and sliced
½ teaspoon dried basil (our host used
  fresh, of course)
1 tablespoon fresh chopped parsley
salt and freshly-ground black pepper

Heat the oil in a large flameproof casserole and fry the onion and garlic over a medium heat for 3–4 minutes. Remove with a draining spoon. Fry the potato slices in batches, removing them to keep warm when they are dry and golden brown. Return the onion and garlic to the casserole with the tomatoes and herbs. Season well and add the potato slices. Simmer over a low heat, stirring occasionally, for 10–15 minutes, until the tomato sauce is dry. Add a very little water during the cooking if the sauce dries before the potatoes are tender—this can happen if under-ripe tomatoes are used or the heat is too high.

Serve in Greek style with a mixed salad sprinkled with crumbled cheese. I have also served a salad of anchovies and black olives—more delicious still—or cooked, green haricot beans with olive oil dressing.

Serves 4

Corn Cakes

I make huge batches of these fritters to serve with fried or roast chicken—batches huge enough to leave some for lunch or supper next day. They are an ideal hot snack, too, for a children's or teenage party.

100 g (4 oz) cornmeal
½ teaspoon baking powder
1 teaspoon sugar
salt and freshly-ground black pepper
2 eggs, separated

150 ml (¼ pint) milk
350 g (12 oz) corn kernels, cooked
(or use canned kernels, drained)
50 g (2 oz) butter

Sift together the cornmeal, baking powder, sugar, salt and pepper into a bowl and make a batter, beating in the egg yolks and milk. Add the drained corn kernels. Whisk the egg whites until stiff and fold them into the mixture.

Melt the butter in a heavy frying pan and, when it is hot, drop in the batter from a tablespoon. When the undersides are golden brown flip the fritters over with a spatula and brown the other side. For a party, provide paper napkins so that guests can eat the fritters with their fingers.

Serves 4

Broad Bean Grill

I like to have a number of broad bean recipes to turn to, because most years we grow so many that they line one wall of the freezer. This one, combining the vegetables with crisp bacon and a creamy sauce, is a favourite.

100 g (4 oz) streaky bacon, without
* rind, chopped*
40 g (1½ oz) butter
40 g (1½ oz) flour
300 ml (½ pint) chicken stock (see
* page 24)*
300 ml (½ pint) single cream or milk

50 g (2 oz) cheese, grated
salt and freshly-ground black pepper
pinch of cayenne pepper
675 g (1½ lb) broad beans, shelled
* and cooked*
25 g (1 oz) crumbled corn flakes
parsley sprigs to garnish

Fry the bacon in a small pan until crisp and dry. Pour off the fat (be sure to reserve it) and remove the bacon pieces. Melt the butter in the cleaned pan, add the flour and stir until well blended and a roux is formed. Gradually stir in the chicken stock—preferably hot—and then the cream or milk. Bring to simmering point, still stirring. Remove the pan from the heat, add half the cheese and season well with salt and pepper. Cook the sauce for 3 minutes, then stir in the bacon and broad beans. Pour into an ovenproof dish to serve and top with the remaining cheese mixed with crumbled corn flakes. Dribble the bacon fat over the top and brown under the grill. Decorate with parsley sprigs.

Serves 4

Courgette Cream

I am indebted to a friend for this recipe. She invited a crowd of us back to her house for 'a snack' when we had been canvassing, and produced a huge dish of courgettes as if by magic. She told us later that we were all too busy warming our hands by the fire to notice the 20 minutes or so it took to cook the prepared dish.

50 g (2 oz) butter
1 large onion, peeled and sliced
2 large cloves garlic, peeled and
* crushed*
675 g (1½ lb) courgettes, trimmed
* and sliced*
½ teaspoon dried basil

1 teaspoon fresh chopped parsley
salt and freshly-ground black pepper
4 eggs
150 ml (¼ pint) single cream
75 g (3 oz) cheese, grated
pinch of cayenne pepper

Melt the butter in a large, heavy pan or frying pan and sauté the onion and garlic for 3–4 minutes over a moderate heat. Add the courgettes and cook until they are golden brown. (This is important, to seal the moisture into the vegetable.) Add the herbs and season well with salt and pepper. Turn into a 900-ml (1½-pint) pie dish or deep gratin dish.

Beat the eggs and cream together, stir in the grated cheese and season with salt and a pinch of cayenne pepper.

Pour the custard mixture over the vegetables, stand the dish on a baking sheet and cook at 180°C (350°F)/Gas 4, for 20–25 minutes, until the custard has set and is light brown on top.

Serve with hot, crusty rolls or rye bread.

Serves 4

Scone Pizza

The Italians have their own ideas about one-pot cooking. With a satisfying base of yeast or scone dough they pile on cheese, tomatoes, anchovies,

peppers, olives—you name it—and serve it straight from the pan. This scone dough is quick and easy to make and a good substitute for the traditional bread dough.

For the scone base:
225 g (8 oz) self-raising flour
1 teaspoon baking powder
¼ teaspoon salt
¼ teaspoon freshly-ground black
  pepper
¼ teaspoon mixed dried herbs
25 g (1 oz) butter, softened
150 ml (¼ pint) milk

For the filling:
450 g (1 lb) ripe tomatoes, skinned
  and sliced
¼ teaspoon dried basil
½ teaspoon salt
¼ teaspoon freshly-ground black
  pepper
1 teaspoon caster sugar
225 g (8 oz) strong Cheddar cheese,
  grated
1 green pepper, trimmed and sliced
1 small can anchovy fillets
14 stuffed green olives, halved

To make the scone base, sift together the flour, baking powder, salt and pepper. Add the herbs and rub in the butter. Pour in just enough milk to make a soft dough. Turn out on to a lightly-floured board and roll to a 25-cm (10-in) circle. Slide into a greased flan tin, heatproof gratin dish or on to a baking sheet. Arrange the tomato slices in rings on top of the dough and sprinkle them with dried basil, salt, pepper and sugar. Scatter with grated cheese and make a lattice pattern with the green pepper slices and anchovy fillets. Fill in the spaces with olives. Bake at 220°C (425°F)/Gas 7, for 25–30 minutes, until the cheese has melted and the scone base is golden brown.

Serves 6

Stuffed Tomatoes and Pimientos

At one of my favourite restaurants guests are always greeted by a waiter holding a tray of stuffed tomatoes and peppers, alternating red and green, like edible traffic lights. I can never wait to get my coat off and begin!

You can serve these vegetables either cold or hot, as a starter or a main course. The same filling can be used for courgettes or aubergines.

6 large tomatoes
6 green or red peppers
2 medium-sized onions, peeled and
  grated
2 cloves garlic, peeled and crushed
1 tablespoon sultanas
½ teaspoon dried basil

100 g (4 oz) button mushrooms,
  wiped and finely chopped
about 125–175 g (5–6 oz) rice,
  cooked (will then weigh about
  450 g (1 lb))
6 tablespoons olive oil
salt and freshly-ground black pepper

Veal Seville (page 95)

Cut the tops off the tomatoes and scoop the flesh into a bowl. Cut the tops off the peppers, trim away the pith and seeds and wash under a tap. Add the onion, garlic, sultanas, basil, mushrooms and cooked rice to the tomato flesh and blend with 2 tablespoons olive oil, seasoning well. Pack the mixture into the tomatoes and peppers. Put the 'lids' back on top and stand the vegetables in a shallow baking dish small enough to stop them from falling over. Pour over about 4 tablespoons olive oil and cover with household foil. Bake at 190°C (375°F)/Gas 5, for 30–35 minutes, removing the foil for the last 10 minutes so that the vegetables brown on top. Serve hot in the baking dish or transfer to another dish and garnish with parsley sprigs to serve cold.

Serves 6

Andros Marrow

I first ate this dish on the Greek Island of Andros, after a three-hour climb to a nunnery. And I first cooked it at 7 o'clock one morning, before the sun was too hot, under the watchful eye of Maria. No wonder I went back to stay in her house twice in that one year!

1 medium–large marrow (to allow 8 slices)	*freshly-ground black pepper*
2 tablespoons good olive oil	*3 heaped tablespoons fresh chopped mint*
1 large onion, peeled and grated	*50 g (2 oz) Wensleydale cheese,*
600 ml (1 pint) water, boiling	*crumbled into small cubes*
175 g (6 oz) long-grain rice	*8 vine leaves (optional but*
1 teaspoon salt	*important)*

I was fascinated to watch Maria prepare the marrow, as deftly as one would core an apple. Chop a small slice from each end and, using a melon baller, scoop out all the seeds and veins. Work from each end until the marrow is hollow but has good, firm walls. Trim the cut-off slices to make 'plugs' to push in the ends, then set aside. Put the olive oil, grated onion and water into a flameproof dish, bring to the boil and simmer for 10 minutes. Add the rice, salt, pepper and mint, cover and cook over a low heat for about 35 minutes. When the rice has absorbed all the water, stir in the cheese and allow the mixture to cool a little.

Plug one end of the marrow with one of the trimmed slices and, using a dessertspoon, pack in the filling. Plug the other end.

Spread 4 vine leaves (if used) over the base of the cleaned dish and set the marrow on top. If you have any filling left over, pack it into a small heatproof bowl and stand it beside the marrow or make into rice cakes (see next recipe). Cover with vine leaves and pour on about 600 ml (1 pint) of water.

Cover the dish and bake at 180°C (350°F)/Gas 4, for 35–40 minutes. Serve with sliced button mushrooms tossed in melted butter.

Serves 4

Rice Cakes

It is difficult to estimate the exact amount of rice filling you will need for a marrow, or other vegetables—it depends how much you scoop out! If you have been over-generous, be thankful. Any left-over rice filling or risotto can be served as rissoles, delicious and crunchy and unusual.

left-over rice filling	*butter*
fresh white breadcrumbs	*Parmesan cheese, grated*

Mould the rice mixture into hamburger shapes. Spread the breadcrumbs on a large sheet of greaseproof paper and coat the rissoles thoroughly, lifting up the edges of the paper to toss the crumbs over the top surface. Melt some butter in a heavy frying pan (about 50 g (2 oz) for 6–8 rissoles) and gently fry the rice cakes for 4 minutes on each side. Serve liberally sprinkled with Parmesan cheese.

Vegetable Pilaff

Here's another recipe, rich in flavour, that makes use of left-over cooked rice. It's a vegetarian dish, but there's plenty of protein—calories, too!—in the peanut garnish.

2 medium-sized aubergines	*100 g (4 oz) button mushrooms,*
salt	*wiped and sliced*
4 tablespoons olive oil	*6 tomatoes, skinned and quartered*
2 medium-sized onions, peeled and	*juice of ½ lemon, strained*
sliced	*freshly-ground black pepper*
1 clove garlic, peeled and finely	*1 tablespoon fresh chopped parsley*
chopped	*to garnish*
1 red pepper, trimmed and sliced	*50 g (2 oz) salted peanuts to*
675 g (1½ lb) cooked rice (from	*garnish*
225 g (8 oz) unpolished rice)	

Dice the aubergines without peeling, sprinkle them with salt and leave in a colander for ½ hour to drain away the bitterness. Rinse under cold water and pat dry on kitchen paper. Heat the oil in a heavy pan and lightly fry the onion and garlic for 4–5 minutes; add the red pepper and then, after 2–3 minutes, the diced aubergine. Cook for a further 4 minutes, then stir in the rice and

119

mushrooms. When these are well blended and coated with oil, stir in the tomatoes and lemon juice and season well with salt and pepper. Cook for a further 2–3 minutes. Pile on to a heated serving dish, sprinkle with chopped parsley and scatter the peanuts over.

Serves 4

Chinese Fried Rice

The Chinese know well the value offered by the 'exploded bulk' of cooked rice—which finishes at about three times its original weight. They also know exactly how to cook each ingredient for only as long as it needs to retain its crispness and character. Left-over cooked rice can be used for this recipe.

2 tablespoons oil
1 large onion, peeled and chopped
1 clove garlic, peeled and finely chopped
2 pieces preserved stem ginger, washed and chopped
1 small green pepper, trimmed and chopped
100 g (4 oz) mushrooms, wiped and chopped

1 225-g (8-oz) can bamboo shoots, drained and sliced
450 g (1 lb) fresh beansprouts, or use canned ones, drained
100 g (4 oz) rice, cooked (will then weigh about 350 g (12 oz))
1 tablespoon soy sauce
salt and freshly-ground black pepper
100 g (4 oz) blanched almonds, shredded

Heat the oil in a heavy pan and fry the onion and garlic over a medium heat for 2–3 minutes before adding all the other vegetables. Stir for 3 minutes before adding the rice, soy sauce and salt and pepper. Allow the rice to heat through, then pile on a heated serving dish and scatter the almonds on top.

Serves 4

Spinach Risotto

In this recipe spinach purée colours a dish of rice yet still leaves each separate grain crisp and dry.

50 g (2 oz) butter
2 tablespoons olive oil
450 g (1 lb) spinach, washed, spines removed, and chopped
1 medium-sized onion, peeled and chopped

2 stalks celery, washed and chopped
450 ml (¾ pint) chicken stock (see page 24)
salt and freshly-ground black pepper
225 g (8 oz) unpolished Italian rice
75 g (3 oz) Parmesan cheese, grated

Heat 25 g (1 oz) butter and the olive oil in a saucepan and add the spinach, onion and celery. Moisten with 2 tablespoons of the stock and season with salt and pepper. Cook over low heat for 15–20 minutes, stirring occasionally with a wooden spoon. When the spinach has collapsed, purée in a mouli mill, an electric blender, or rub through a sieve. Put the stock in the pan, add the rice and the purée and stir well. Simmer for 20–25 minutes, until the rice has absorbed all the stock, adding a little more if it dries out too quickly. Stir in the remaining butter and half the Parmesan cheese. Serve on a hot dish sprinkled with the remaining cheese. A tomato, onion and basil salad is a good accompaniment.

Serves 4

Spinach Pie

Filo, or leaf, pastry is best for this dish. You can buy it in some delicatessens, but if not in yours, substitute bought puff pastry and roll it as thin as possible—until you can see through it.

900 g (2 lb) spinach, stems removed and well washed	*1 tablespoon fresh chopped parsley*
25 g (1 oz) butter	*2 eggs, beaten*
6 spring onions, white part only, trimmed and sliced	*225 g (8 oz) feta cheese (if not available, use Wensleydale)*
1 tablespoon fresh chopped dill leaves or 1 dessertspoon dried dill leaves.	*salt and freshly-ground black pepper*
	olive oil
	450 g (1 lb) filo or puff pastry

Chop the spinach leaves. Melt the butter in a large pan and add the spring onions. Sauté for 2–3 minutes over a medium heat, then add the spinach and stir well. Cover and cook for 2–3 minutes until it collapses. Remove the lid and cook until the water has evaporated. Take the pan from the heat. When the spinach is cool add the herbs, beaten eggs and crumbled cheese and season well with salt and pepper.

Brush a gingerbread tin with olive oil. Cut the filo pastry in sheets to fit the tin. Brushing between each layer with olive oil, use half the pastry in layers over the base of the tin. Spread the spinach mixture on top and cover with the remaining pastry sheets, again brushing each layer with olive oil. (If using puff pastry, use half to cover the base of the tin and the remainder on top. No oil is of course required.) Push the pastry firmly against the sides of the pan and trim the edges. Brush the top liberally with oil. Bake at 180°C (350°F)/ Gas 4, for ½ hour. Reduce the heat to 150°C (300°F)/Gas 2, and bake for a further ½ hour, until the top is golden brown and the pastry is well risen. Serve hot, cut in squares, or cold in small fingers, with drinks.

Serves 8

Watercress Lattice Flan

Watercress makes a refreshing filling for an open flan; serve this as a meal in itself or a delicious starter to a dinner party.

shortcrust pastry made with 225 g
  (8 oz) flour etc. (see page 73)
2 bunches watercress, trimmed and
  washed
50 g (2 oz) cheese, grated
175 g (6 oz) cottage cheese, sieved

25 g (1 oz) shelled walnuts,
  chopped
100 g (4 oz) mushrooms, wiped and
  sliced
2 eggs, beaten
salt and freshly-ground black pepper
milk to glaze

Stand a 20-cm (8-in) flan ring on a baking sheet and line it with three-quarters of the pastry. Trim the edges. Poach the watercress in a little boiling salted water for 4 minutes, drain, pat dry on kitchen paper and chop. Sprinkle grated cheese over the flan base and cover with the watercress. Mix together the cottage cheese, walnuts and mushrooms. Stir in the beaten eggs and season with salt and pepper. Pour over the watercress. Cut the remaining pastry into pencil-thin strips and lay in a lattice pattern on top of the flan. Trim and seal the edges. Brush the pastry with a little milk, and bake the flan at 180°C (350°F)/Gas 4, for 40 minutes, until the pastry is golden brown. Serve warm.

Serves 4–6

Cheese Meringue Flan

The creaminess of cheese meringue makes a delicious topping to a savoury flan. Try the same topping on fish flans, too. It's delicious.

1 18-cm (7-in) shortcrust flan case,
  cooked
25 g (1 oz) butter
25 g (1 oz) flour
300 ml (½ pint) milk
175 g (6 oz) mushrooms, wiped and
  sliced
2 egg yolks

1 dessertspoon fresh chopped parsley
salt and freshly-ground black pepper

For the topping:
2 egg whites
pinch of salt
50 g (2 oz) cheese, grated
paprika pepper to garnish

Make a white sauce with the butter, flour and milk, remove the pan from the heat and add the mushrooms, reserving a few slices to garnish. Mix in the egg yolks and parsley and season with salt and pepper. Pour the mushroom sauce into the pastry case.

    To make the topping, whisk the egg whites and salt until stiff, then fold in the cheese. Spread this meringue mixture over the case. Bake at 180°C (350°F)/Gas 4, for 20 minutes. Allow to cool, arrange the reserved mushroom slices on top and sprinkle sparingly with paprika pepper to garnish. Serve cold with salad.

Serves 4–6

Cheese Pudding

Blue-vein cheese it is, and blue-vein cheese it tastes like. But, in cooking, the veins disappear and the pudding is a creamy golden colour.

50 g (2 oz) butter	*salt and freshly-ground black pepper*
1 medium-sized onion, peeled and chopped	*4 large eggs, separated*
50 g (2 oz) flour	*50 g (2 oz) fresh white breadcrumbs*
300 ml (½ pint) milk, warm	*½ teaspoon Worcestershire sauce*
100 g (4 oz) Danish blue cheese	*2 tablespoons fresh chopped parsley*

Melt the butter in a saucepan and sauté the onion over a moderate heat for 3 minutes until soft. Add the flour, stir to make a roux and gradually pour in the milk, stirring until the sauce boils. Continue simmering for 2–3 minutes. Remove the pan from the heat and crumble in the cheese. Season well with salt and pepper and beat in the egg yolks. Stir in the breadcrumbs, Worcestershire sauce and chopped parsley. Whisk the egg whites until stiff and fold into the mixture with a metal spoon.

Pour into a greased 1·2-litre (2-pint) pie dish, stand on a baking sheet and cook at 190°C (375°F)/Gas 5, for 30 minutes until the pudding has risen and is firm to touch. Serve with a crisp green salad.

Serves 4

Potato Rösti

Served straight from the pan, this dish has always seemed to me to be in the spirit of Bonfire Nights, or a Hallowe'en party. But there's certainly no need to wait for those occasions to enjoy it.

25 g (1 oz) butter	*50 g (2 oz) cheese, grated*
50 g (2 oz) bacon, without rind, chopped	*¼ teaspoon dry mustard*
1 large onion, peeled and finely sliced	*salt and freshly-ground black pepper*
675 g (1½ lb) potatoes, boiled	*¼ teaspoon dried thyme*
	fat for frying

Melt the butter in a heavy frying pan or a flameproof serving dish over a moderate heat. Fry the bacon and onion for 2–3 minutes. Grate the cooked potatoes into a large bowl and add the bacon, onion, cheese, dry mustard, salt, pepper and herb. Add a knob of lard to the frying pan and when it is smoking hot turn the potato mixture into the pan. Smooth it out with a palette knife and fry for 5–6 minutes until golden brown on the underside. Flip the pancake over and fry until the other side is the same colour. Serve from the pan with spiced chutney.

Serves 4

Rainbow Mousse

Colourful with carrot and watercress, this mousse makes an attractive dish for a warm summer evening, or, in larger quantities, a centrepiece for a buffet. It's a cheat, really, as it requires no cooking.

2 bunches of watercress, trimmed, washed and finely chopped (reserve a few sprigs to garnish)
350 g (12 oz) carrots, peeled or scraped and grated
2 spring onions, trimmed and finely chopped

grated rind and juice of 1 lemon
1 150-g (5-oz) carton natural yoghurt
2 eggs, separated
salt and freshly-ground black pepper
15 g (½ oz) gelatine

In a large bowl, combine the chopped watercress, grated carrot, spring onion and lemon rind. Stir in the lemon juice, yoghurt and egg yolks and season well with salt and pepper. Sprinkle the gelatine in 3 tablespoons of water in a cup and stand in a bowl of hot water to dissolve. Allow to cool, then pour into the watercress mixture and stir well. Whisk the egg whites until stiff and fold into the mixture, using a metal spoon. Pour the mousse into a wetted 900-ml (1½-pint) mould and leave in a cool place to set. Run a sharp knife round the edge of the mould and invert on a plate to turn out. Decorate with sprigs of watercress.

Serves 4–6

STEAMING AWAY

In Britain, we have our own excellent one-pot cooking method, the steamed pudding, which encases mixtures of meat, fish, vegetables or fruit in the lightest, airiest of pastries, suet crust. Whether it is used to line and cover a pudding basin or rolled round the filling to form a sausage shape, suet pastry is one of the easiest to make, and rewards attention to a few details in the preparation with a texture approaching that of a whisked sponge cake.

The most traditional of all English steamed puddings, of course, is beef steak and kidney pudding, the dish that cooks in top restaurants and homes throughout the country serve with justifiable national pride. With so much goodness trapped in one dish, there is little need for anything more—just one plain green vegetable, perhaps, and fresh fruit to follow. One-pot cooking *par excellence.*

Before getting down to the basic suet crust recipe, and the selection of fillings that follow, it is perhaps as well to brush up on a few general points that will enable you to make your puddings rank with the best in the land.

Firstly, the choice of suet. Packet suets are reliable and give good results. The granules are lightly coated with rice flour which keeps them separate, prevents them from mixing into a sticky glob, and helps even mixing. If you prefer to buy suet from the butcher, and grate it yourself—which is cheaper, of course—choose beef kidney suet, which has a firmer, crisper texture than others and grates more finely. Remove every trace of skin first, cut out any discoloured parts and use a medium grater. Imitate the packet products and shake the grated suet in a little of the weighed flour before proceeding with the recipe.

If you do not have any suet to hand, or want to use another fat, you can produce similar results with cooking fat, dripping or lard. Use the block of fat straight from the refrigerator or a very cold place and grate it finely. A recipe is also given for a richer butter crust which, with the addition of beaten egg yolks, makes a softer, more golden pastry.

Now, for the lightness of texture that will distinguish your pudding from the wedges of stodge one remembers from school. Much as some traditional

126

cooks deplore the idea (country people I know refer to it as 'they artificials'), an artificial raising agent added to the flour is essential for good aeration. It is the acid and alkaline content in the baking powder that gives the pastry the characteristic lift. Use self-raising flour if you have it, with the raising agent well sifted and blended throughout the flour; and if you like you can sift in a further teaspoon of baking powder to each 225 g (8 oz) flour. If you use plain flour, add baking powder in the proportion of 3 level teaspoons to 225 g (8 oz) of flour and make sure that it is well distributed.

Breadcrumbs, too, can help the texture and for an even lighter crust, try substituting up to half the quantity of flour with the same weight of freshly-grated white breadcrumbs. This flour-breadcrumb mixture is the one used for steamed chocolate, lemon and other sweet puddings, as well as for a variation of suet crust.

As with all types of pastry, suet crust benefits from light handling. When you have made the dough, turn it out on to a lightly-floured board and knead it gently with your knuckles until the dough forms a smooth paste. Don't work off the day's worries and frustrations by continuing to pull and punch the dough, or you will have one more worry on your hands—tough suet crust into the bargain. After kneading, cover the dough with a clean tea towel and allow it to relax and 'breathe' for 5–10 minutes. At the rolling stage, continue to handle the dough as if it were something delicate and precious, which it is, and avoid stretching it with rough, rapid movements. Roll it to a thickness of about 1 cm ($\frac{1}{2}$ in).

Well grease the basin first, so that you will be able to make a neat job of serving the pudding. Divide up the pastry, two-thirds to line the basin and the remainder for the lid. Roll out the main piece to a circle 5 cm (2 in) larger than the diameter of the top of the basin. Lightly dust it all over with flour and fold in half, then in half again, so that you have a triangular shape. Lightly roll over the pastry towards the point of the triangle to lengthen it slightly, then lower it inside the basin. Unfold the pastry and mould it with your fingers to fit. Pour in the filling—which should always be cool—then turn a lip of the pastry over, all round the edge. Brush this with water, roll the lid exactly to fit and lower it on top. Trim round the edge with a sharp knife and pinch to seal the edge well.

Cover the basin with a piece of greased greaseproof paper or kitchen foil, making a pleat across the centre to allow the pudding to rise. Pinch foil down all round, under the basin rim, so that it fits well, or tie greaseproof paper with string under the rim. If you are to boil the pudding, that is to say, stand it in boiling water rather than place it in a steamer over a pan of boiling water, cover the basin with a further layer—a scalded pudding cloth of unbleached calico, tied firmly under the rim with string, is just right. Knot the ends above the pudding so that you can lift it out of the water easily.

For a less filling pudding, you can halve the quantity of suet-crust or butter-crust pastry used. Grease a 900-ml ($1\frac{1}{2}$-pint) pudding basin, put in the filling, then press on a thick round of pastry crust to form a lid.

To make a suet-crust roll, with a meat or sweet filling, spread the filling across a rectangle of the pastry to within 2·5 cm (1 in) of the edges, brush them all along with water and roll up like a sausage. Pinch the edges firmly with your fingers to seal. Place the roll in the centre of a piece of household foil, make a pleat to allow the pastry to expand, then wrap it round and twist the ends firmly to seal. The pastry will be spoiled if you leave any holes for the steam to attack.

The length of time needed for cooking depends on the filling, not the pastry, which will not spoil with long cooking. Most meat puddings should be steamed for 3–4 hours or boiled for 2–$2\frac{1}{2}$ hours, until the meat is tender and the gravy thick and rich. The cooking time can be cut down, however, by pressure cooking—a positive boon for all steamed puddings—or by pre-cooking the filling in a saucepan or casserole. If you do this, let it cool thoroughly before pouring it into the pudding crust, otherwise the crust will turn soggy. Fruit puddings need only about $1\frac{1}{2}$–2 hours' steaming or 1–$1\frac{1}{2}$ hours' boiling and no pre-cooking of the filling. This is a sure way to lose both flavour and texture.

To boil a pudding, select a saucepan which allows a space of at least 2·5 cm (1 in) all round the top of the basin. A closer fit than this, and the top of the pudding will not be properly cooked. Place a trivet in the pan, pour in boiling water to come about half-way up the basin, cover and allow the water to return to the boil. Only then should you put in the pudding. Cover the pan with a lid or a heatproof glass plate, so that you can see when the water needs topping up, and keep the water boiling all the time. For steaming put the basin in a steamer, cover with the lid and place over a pan of boiling water.

Some cooks are shy of serving a meat pudding in the basin in which it was cooked, but this is the traditional and accepted way to do it. Wrap a coloured or gingham napkin round the basin and bring the pudding proudly to the table on a large plate or serving dish. Cut the pudding into wedges, keeping the filling intact if possible. Fruit puddings, on the other hand, are always turned out of the basin and cut into slices. Because of this, it is important to pack the filling well into the crust, to make the pudding stand good and firm.

Suet-crust Pastry

To achieve a lighter crust, make up the weight of flour with equal amounts of flour and breadcrumbs. It is worth remembering that the amount of shredded suet you use is always half the weight of the flour, or flour and breadcrumbs.

*350 g (12 oz) self-raising flour plus
1 heaped teaspoon baking powder
(optional) or 350 g (12 oz) plain
flour plus 4–4½ level teaspoons
baking powder*

*½ teaspoon salt
175 g (6 oz) shredded or grated suet
little cold water to mix*

Sift the flour, baking powder if used, and salt together in a bowl, add the shredded suet and mix well. Gradually pour in the water, mixing with a palette knife or round-bladed knife, until all the flour is absorbed. This should take 150 ml (¼ pint) water at the most.

Lightly flour a pastry board, turn the dough on to it and knead lightly with your knuckles until there are no more cracks in the dough. Shape it into a ball and wrap it in a clean tea towel. Leave to rest for 5–10 minutes.

Roll out the pastry with a rolling pin also lightly dusted with flour. Take care not to damage or stretch the pastry as you work, and roll it to an even thickness of about 1 cm (½ in).

This quantity is enough to line and cover a 1·2-litre (2-pint) pudding basin. Halve the amount if you want to use it just as a thick crust on top of the pudding basin, or to top a casserole.

Butter-crust Pastry

*350 g (12 oz) self-raising flour plus
1 heaped teaspoon baking powder
(optional) or 350 g (12 oz) plain
flour plus 4–4½ teaspoons baking
powder*

*½ teaspoon salt
115 g (4½ oz) butter, straight from
 refrigerator
3 egg yolks, well beaten
little water*

Sift the flour, baking powder if used and salt into a bowl. Grate the butter and mix into the flour. Bind with beaten egg yolks and add only enough cold water to make a firm pliable dough. Knead, leave to rest and roll out as for suet-crust pastry. This quantity is enough to line and cover a 1·2-litre (2-pint) pudding basin. Reduce the quantity if you prefer to use the crust just as a thick, golden lid to a pudding basin or casserole.

Steak and Kidney Pudding

I have sometimes thought that if we in Britain have a poor reputation for cooking, we have only ourselves to blame. If we served our foreign visitors with traditional steak and kidney pudding, they would go home dissatisfied with their own national cuisine, not ours!

suet-crust pastry (see page 128)
225 g (8 oz) sheep's kidney, skinned
· and cored
1 heaped tablespoon flour
salt and freshly-ground black pepper
675 g (1½ lb) steak, trimmed and cut
into cubes
1 large onion, peeled and finely
chopped

100 g (4 oz) field mushrooms,
washed, peeled and sliced
300 ml (½ pint) brown bone stock
(see page 22) or 150 ml (¼ pint)
stock and 150 ml (¼ pint) cheap
port
1 teaspoon mushroom ketchup or soy
sauce (optional)

Make the suet-crust pastry and line a greased 1·2-litre (2-pint) pudding basin
as described. If you want to blanch the kidney, do so for 1 minute in boiling
water, then pat dry on kitchen paper. Cut the kidney into small cubes. Put the
flour in a polythene bag, add salt and pepper and the cubes of steak and
kidney. Shake well until the meat is coated with flour. Combine the meat,
onion and mushrooms and put them into the basin. Combine the stock (or
stock and port) and ketchup or sauce, if used, and pour over the meat. Place
the pastry lid on top of the basin and seal the edge. Cover as described and
steam for 3½–4 hours.

Serves 4–6

Steak and Oyster Pudding *(photograph facing page 132)*

Here's a dish fit to set before visiting royalty, if ever there was one! I first
enjoyed this pudding in one of London's marvellously old-fashioned
restaurants. The chef had used fresh oysters, but I hope he will forgive me for
substituting canned ones.

suet-crust pastry (see page 128)
225 g (8 oz) ox kidney, skinned and
blanched if wished
1 heaped tablespoon flour
salt and freshly-ground black pepper
pinch of cayenne pepper
675 g (1½ lb) chuck steak, trimmed
and cut into cubes

1 small can oysters
175 g (6 oz) field mushrooms,
washed, peeled and sliced
1 teaspoon Worcestershire sauce
1 small wineglass medium sherry
150 ml (¼ pint) brown bone stock
(see page 22)

Make the suet-crust pastry and line a greased 1·2-litre (2-pint) pudding basin
as described. If you've blanched the kidney, pat it dry; then chop into small
cubes. Put the flour, salt and pepper into a polythene bag, add the pieces of
steak and kidney and shake until they are well covered with flour. Drain the
oysters and reserve the liquor. Combine the meat with the mushrooms and
oysters and put into the lined basin. Combine the oyster liquor with the

Worcestershire sauce, sherry and stock and pour over the meat. Cover with the pastry lid, seal the edge and cover as described. Steam for $3\frac{1}{2}$–4 hours.

Serves 4–6

Beef and Anchovy Pudding

When I served this pudding flavoured with anchovies and pickled walnuts, someone in my family asked what's wrong with good old steak and kidney. Nothing! But some cooks like to experiment occasionally . . . .

suet-crust pastry (see page 128)
675 g (1½ lb) beef skirt, trimmed
 and cut into cubes
50 g (2 oz) lean ham, cut into cubes
1 tablespoon flour
freshly-ground black pepper
1 teaspoon dried marjoram

pinch each of ground cloves, mace
 and nutmeg
3 anchovy fillets, pounded
2 pickled walnuts, finely chopped
1 wineglass cheap port
150 ml (¼ pint) brown bone stock
 (see page 22)

Make the suet-crust pastry and line a greased 1·2-litre (2-pint) pudding basin as described. Toss the beef and ham in the flour seasoned with pepper, the marjoram and the other spices. Combine with the pounded anchovy and chopped walnut and pack lightly into the lined pudding basin. Mix the port wine with the stock and pour over the meat. Place the pastry lid on the basin, seal the edge and cover as described. Steam for 4 hours.

Serves 4

Elizabethan Pudding

If you ever feel sore about the way we have to economise nowadays, take heart. This pudding, which consists of little more than minced beef and bacon, was served at many an Elizabethan banquet.

suet-crust pastry (see page 128)
100 g (4 oz) bacon, without rind,
 chopped
350 g (12 oz) minced beef
100 g (4 oz) pig's kidney, skinned,
 cored and blanched if wished

2 tablespoons flour
salt and freshly-ground black pepper
1 small onion, finely chopped
2 large tomatoes, skinned and sliced
scant 300 ml (½ pint) brown bone
 stock (see page 22)

Make the suet-crust pastry and line a greased 1·2-litre (2-pint) pudding basin as described. Shake the bacon, minced meat and chopped kidney in the flour, well seasoned with salt and pepper. Combine with the onion and tomato and pack into the lined pudding basin. Pour on just enough stock to cover the meat (the filling should be thick and solid when the pudding is cooked). Cover the basin with the pastry lid, seal the edge and cover with greased greaseproof paper or foil as described. Steam for 2–2½ hours.

Serves 4

Liver and Tomato Pudding

This rich, red pudding looks as welcoming as glowing coals in the hearth. But it *is* rich; serve it with only a green vegetable such as curly kale or cabbage or a crisp winter salad.

suet-crust pastry (see page 128) to which you have added 1 teaspoon mixed dried herbs
2 tablespoons flour
salt and freshly-ground black pepper
1 teaspoon dried oregano
1 tablespoon fresh chopped parsley

450 g (1 lb) lamb's liver, washed, dried and chopped
1 medium-sized onion, peeled and chopped
1 225-g (8-oz) can tomatoes
1 tablespoon tomato purée
1 tablespoon Worcestershire sauce

Make the suet-crust pastry and line a greased 1·2-litre (2-pint) pudding basin as described. Combine the flour, seasoning and herbs in a polythene bag and add the liver pieces. Shake to coat thoroughly in flour. Combine with the onion and the drained and chopped tomatoes. Blend the tomato purée into the liquor from the can. Put the meat into the lined pudding basin and pour over the tomato liquid and sauce. Cover with the pastry lid, seal the edge and cover as described. Steam for 3½–4 hours.

Serves 4

'Goose' Pudding

The combination of liver, heart and bacon is said to resemble the flavour of goose. Even if your imagination doesn't travel that far, it's a pleasant filling for a pudding with, this time, only a lid of suet-crust pastry.

suet-crust pastry (see page 128, and halve recipe)
675 g (1½ lb) lamb's liver, cut into cubes
1 lamb's heart, cleaned and cut into cubes
225 g (8 oz) bacon, in the piece, rind removed, then diced
1 tablespoon flour

salt and freshly-ground black pepper
¼ teaspoon dried sage
1 teaspoon fresh chopped parsley
grated rind of ½ lemon
2 large onions, peeled and sliced
1 large potato, peeled and sliced
150 ml (¼ pint) white stock (see page 31)

Steak and Oyster Pudding (page 130)

Grease a 1·2-litre (2-pint) pudding basin, make the suet-crust pastry as described and roll it out to fit the top of the basin, as a lid. Set aside until needed. Shake the pieces of liver, heart and bacon in the flour seasoned with salt, pepper, herbs and lemon rind. Put the meat, onion and potato in the greased pudding basin and pour on the stock. Lay the pastry lid on top of the meat mixture, pressing it well against the side. Cover the basin as described and steam for 3 hours.

Serves 4–6

Pork and Apple Pudding

The great advantage of this pudding—apart from the delicious richness—is that you can make it with a cheap cut of meat, and no one will know.

suet-crust pastry (see page 128, and use 75 g (3 oz) self-raising flour and 75 g (3 oz) fresh white breadcrumbs)
675 g (1½ lb) lean belly of pork, minced
2 rashers of lean bacon, without rind, minced
salt and freshly-ground black pepper

½ teaspoon dried sage, or 1 teaspoon fresh chopped herb
2 medium-sized onions, peeled and chopped
1 teaspoon soft dark brown sugar
450 g (1 lb) russet eating apples, peeled, cored and sliced
150 ml (¼ pint) dry cider

Make the suet-crust pastry as described and roll out to a thick circle to fit the top of greased 1·2-litre (2-pint) pudding basin. Mix together the minced pork and bacon, seasoning, onion and sugar. Put layers of the meat mixture and apples in the pudding basin and pour on the cider. Cover with the pastry lid, seal the edges and cover the basin as described. Steam for 2½–3 hours.

Serves 4–6

Chicken Butter-crust Pudding

butter-crust pastry (see page 129)
4 chicken joints, skinned
1 tablespoon flour
salt and freshly-ground black pepper
100 g (4 oz) ham, diced
100 g (4 oz) button mushrooms, wiped and sliced
1 small green pepper, trimmed and thinly sliced

12 small shallots, peeled and blanched in boiling water for 1 minute
1 teaspoon fresh chopped marjoram or ½ teaspoon dried herb
1 teaspoon fresh chopped parsley
300 ml (½ pint) chicken stock (see page 24)

Orange Sunflowers (page 145); Country Cobbler (page 153)   133

Make the butter-crust pastry and line a greased 1·2-litre (2-pint) pudding basin. Toss the skinned chicken joints in the flour, well seasoned with salt and pepper. Put the chicken joints and ham in the lined pudding basin, add the mushrooms, green pepper and the blanched shallots and sprinkle with herbs. Pour on the chicken stock, cover with the pastry lid and seal the edges. Cover the basin as described and steam for 2½–3 hours.

Serves 4

Lamb and Prune Pudding

This pudding is an adaptation of the recipe for Devonshire squab pie, when the lamb chops are cooked whole, peeping through a shortcrust pastry cover.

butter-crust pastry (see page 129)
6 large best-end of neck lamb chops
salt and freshly-ground black pepper
¼ teaspoon freshly-grated nutmeg
pinch of cinnamon
1 teaspoon soft dark brown sugar

900 g (2 lb) russet eating apples, peeled, cored and sliced
1 large onion, peeled and finely chopped
225 g (8 oz) prunes, unsoaked
150 ml (¼ pint) brown bone stock (see page 22)

Make the butter-crust pastry and line a greased 1·2-litre (2-pint) pudding basin. Trim the chops with a sharp knife, discarding the skin and gristle, and stand them, bones upwards, in the lined pudding basin. Mix together the salt, pepper, spices and sugar. Put layers of apple, onion and prunes around the chops, seasoning with the sugar mixture. Pour on the stock, cover with the pastry lid and seal the edges. Cover the basin as described and steam for 2½ hours. To serve, wrap the basin in a napkin as usual and gently push the bone ends through the pastry lid.

Serves 6

Lamb and Bean Pudding

With dried haricot beans, diced vegetables and lamb all wrapped up in suet-crust pastry, surely no one could ask more of a single pot!

100 g (4 oz) dried haricot beans, soaked
suet-crust pastry (see page 128)
450 g (1 lb) lamb, cut in cubes
1 tablespoon flour
salt and freshly-ground black pepper
1 tablespoon fresh chopped parsley

1 large onion, peeled and sliced
1 medium-sized carrot, peeled or scraped and chopped
1 small turnip, peeled and chopped
1 stalk celery, washed and sliced
300 ml (½ pint) white stock (see page 31)

Cover the soaked haricot beans with cold water, bring slowly to the boil and simmer for 1 hour. Drain and allow to cool. Make the suet-crust pastry and line a 1·2-litre (2-pint) pudding basin as described. Toss the cubed lamb in flour seasoned with salt, pepper and parsley. Put the meat and all the vegetables into the lined pudding basin and pour on the stock. Cover with the pastry lid, seal the edge and cover as described. Steam for 3 hours.

Serves 4–6

Rich Hare Pudding

One of the richest of all steamed puddings, this one. It has all the flavour of jugged hare, trapped under the light pudding crust.

For the marinade:
2 tablespoons olive oil
1 wineglass red wine
1 wineglass red wine vinegar
1 shallot, peeled and sliced
1 sprig rosemary
1 bayleaf, crushed
4 juniper berries, crushed
salt and freshly-ground black pepper
6 joints hare

For the pastry:
suet-crust pastry (see page 128, and use 175 g (6 oz) self-raising flour and 175 g (6 oz) fresh white breadcrumbs)

For the filling:
2 tablespoons flour
little salt and freshly-ground black pepper
1 tablespoon fresh chopped parsley
100 g (4 oz) bacon, without rind, cubed
1 stalk celery, washed and chopped
2 small carrots, peeled or scraped and thinly sliced
1 tablespoon redcurrant jelly
150 ml (¼ pint) brown bone stock (see page 22)

Mix together the marinade ingredients, pour them into a shallow dish and add the joints of hare. Leave them to marinate for about 6 hours, or overnight. Turn them occasionally if possible.

Make the suet-crust pastry as described and line a greased 1·2-litre (2-pint) pudding basin.

Lift the hare joints from the marinade, reserving the liquor, and pat them dry. With a very sharp knife, ease the meat away from the bones. Toss the meat in seasoned flour (remember, though, that the marinade is already seasoned), combine with the bacon and vegetables and pack tightly into the lined pudding basin. Stir the redcurrant jelly into the marinade, add the stock and pour over the meat. Cover with the pastry lid, seal the edge and cover as described. Steam for 4½–5 hours, depending on the age of the hare.

Serves 6

Scallop and Mushroom Pudding

Fish in a rich, creamy sauce is a perfect partner for butter-crust pastry, used here as a thick topping only. Serve this dish, which is all golden, buttery coloured, with the greenest of vegetables, broccoli or fresh haricot beans.

butter-crust pastry (see page 129, and make up two-thirds the amount)	*25 g (1 oz) butter*
	25 g (1 oz) flour
	1 small wineglass sweet sherry
8 scallops	*175 g (6 oz) button mushrooms, wiped and sliced*
300 ml (½ pint) milk	
salt and freshly-ground black pepper	*1 tablespoon fresh chopped parsley*

Make the butter-crust pastry as described and roll out to fit the top of a 900-ml (1½-pint) heatproof casserole.

Cut the scallops in half. Put them with the milk in a small saucepan, season with salt and pepper and bring slowly to boiling point. Simmer for 10 minutes. Lift out the scallops with a draining spoon, reserving the milk. Melt the butter in a small pan, stir in the flour, then gradually stir in the reserved milk. Simmer for 3–4 minutes, stirring, then pour in the sherry and blend well. Add the mushrooms, parsley and scallops and taste for seasoning. Add more if needed. Turn the mixture into the casserole and cover with the pastry lid, pressing it well against the sides. Cover the pastry as described and steam for 2 hours. Make sure that there is a clearance of at least 2·5 cm (1 in) all round between the dish and the saucepan.

Serves 4

Bacon Roly-poly

I can't remember any winter when I haven't made at least one bacon roly-poly. It's always for Saturday lunch, on the coldest of days, and served with leeks in béchamel sauce.

suet-crust pastry (see page 128, and make up two-thirds the amount)	*1 small leek, thoroughly washed*
	1 medium-sized onion, peeled and finely chopped
1 teaspoon yeast extract	
225 g (8 oz) streaky bacon, without rind	*freshly-ground black pepper*
	1 tablespoon fresh chopped parsley

Make the suet-crust pastry as described and roll out to an oblong shape about 25 × 20 cm (10 × 8 in). Spread evenly with the yeast extract and cover to within 2·5 cm (1 in) of the edges with the bacon rashers. Chop the white part of the leek finely, discarding the green. Spread the leek and the onion over the bacon. Season well with pepper and sprinkle with the parsley. Dampen the edges of the pastry and roll into a sausage shape, pressing the joins well together, to seal. Make a pleat in the centre of a piece of kitchen foil to allow the pastry to rise. Place the roll in the centre, wrap it up firmly and press the joins well together. Place on a trivet in a pan with a little boiling water and boil for 1½ hours, or cook in a steamer for 2 hours.

In our family, a thin slice is cut from each end of the pudding and given to the birds before anyone else is served!

Serves 4

Beef and Veal Roly-poly

You can vary the filling for a savoury roll, according to what's in the larder. Minced beef with thinly-sliced vegetables, minced beef and bacon together, or minced hare and veal are all good. Use about 225 g (8 oz) meat for a pastry roll made with 225 g (8 oz) self-raising flour.

suet-crust pastry (see page 128, and make up two-thirds the amount)
225 g (8 oz) minced beef and veal mixed
¼ teaspoon dried oregano
1 medium-sized onion, peeled and finely chopped
grated rind ½ lemon
salt and freshly-ground black pepper

Make the suet-crust pastry as described and roll out to an oblong about 25 × 20 cm (10 × 8 in). Mix together the minced meat, herb, onion and lemon rind and seasoning. Spread to within about 2·5 cm (1 in) of the edges of the pastry. Roll up, cover and cook as for Bacon Roly-poly (above).

Serves 4

Faggot Dumplings

So many old-fashioned recipes are well worth a new look. This one, for dumplings stuffed with a liver and bacon mixture, used to be a favourite at the end of a long day on the farm.

550 g (1¼ lb) pigs' liver, minced
4 rashers back bacon, without rind, minced
2 medium-sized onions, peeled and minced
100 g (4 oz) fresh white breadcrumbs
75 g (3 oz) shredded suet
1 teaspoon dried basil
2 teaspoons fresh sage or 1 teaspoon dried herb
salt and freshly-ground black pepper
suet-crust pastry (see page 128; make two-third the amount, and add ¼ teaspoon mixed dried herbs)
600 ml (1 pint) brown bone stock (see page 22)
chopped fresh parsley, to garnish

In a large bowl, mix together all the filling ingredients until they are well blended. Form into 6 equal-sized balls and put them in a small greased baking tin. Bake in the centre of the oven at 180°C (350°F)/Gas 4, for ½ hour, turning once. Remove the faggots from the tin and allow to cool.

Make the suet-crust pastry as described and cut into 6 circles about 10 cm (4 in) across. Dip the faggots in water and wrap each one in a pastry circle. Dampen the edges and pinch to seal.

Bring the stock to the boil and drop in the dumplings. Return to the boil and simmer for 15 minutes. Remove the dumplings with a draining spoon and pile on a heated dish. Sprinkle with chopped parsley and serve with cauliflower or leeks.

Serves 6

Figgy Pudding

I had never tasted fig pudding until one year our carol singing group, at the end of their performance, started to sing the traditional words, 'Now bring us some figgy pudding'. And with great forethought the hostess did! Here is the recipe—in case similar demands are ever made on you.

75 g (3 oz) figs, chopped	*¼ teaspoon salt*
75 g (3 oz) stoneless dates, chopped	*100 g (4 oz) fresh white breadcrumbs*
50 g (2 oz) seedless raisins, chopped	*100 g (4 oz) shredded suet*
2 tablespoons mixed peel, chopped	*50 g (2 oz) soft dark brown sugar*
100 g (4 oz) flour	*1 egg, beaten*
1 teaspoon baking powder	*150 ml (¼ pint) milk*

Grease a 900-ml (1½-pint) pudding basin.

Mix together the chopped fruit and peel. Sieve the flour, baking powder and salt together and stir in the breadcrumbs, shredded suet and sugar. Add the fruit and bind the mixture with the beaten egg and milk. Turn into the pudding basin, cover with greased greaseproof paper or foil for steaming and with a scalded pudding cloth for boiling. Steam for 3½ hours or boil for 2½ hours. Leave the pudding for a minute or two, to shrink slightly, then run a sharp knife round the edge. Turn out of the basin on to a warmed dish. Serve with soured cream.

Serves 4

Steamed Plum Pudding

Not the Christmas-pudding kind of plum pudding—though that would certainly qualify for the one-pot cooking category—but a pudding tangy with russet-coloured autumn plums.

138

suet-crust pastry (see page 128; make two-thirds the amount, and add 1 teaspoon powdered cinnamon)
demerara sugar to dust pudding basin

450 g (1 lb) red plums
225 g (8 oz) cooking apples, peeled, cored and sliced
75 g (3 oz) soft dark brown sugar

Make the suet-crust pastry as described, sifting the cinnamon with the flour. Grease a 900-ml (1½-pint) pudding basin and dust with demerara sugar. Line with two-thirds of the pastry and reserve the rest for the lid. Remove some of the stones from the plums. Leave a few to add to the flavour of the pudding— but warn your guests that you have done so! Pack the plums and apple tightly into the pudding basin, sprinkling with sugar. Cover with the pastry lid, seal the edges and cover as described. Steam for 1½–2 hours. Run a sharp knife between the pudding and the basin to make turning out easier. Turn on to a warmed serving dish and serve hot with whipped cream to which you have added a few pinches of cinnamon.

Serves 4

Whole Lemon Pudding

There's a golden surprise inside this pudding—whole lemons cooked to a glowing softness and as clear as a pot of jelly marmalade.

suet-crust pastry (see page 128; make half the amount, using equal measures of flour and breadcrumbs)

demerara sugar to dust pudding basin
2 small lemons
175 g (6 oz) soft light brown sugar

Make the suet-crust pastry as described. Grease a 600-ml (1-pint) pudding basin and dust with demerara sugar. This gives the pudding a shiny surface when it is turned out. Line the pudding basin with two-thirds of the pastry and reserve the remainder for the lid. Put the two whole lemons in the basin—or, for easier serving, cut them into halves or quarters if you prefer— and sprinkle the light brown sugar round them. Cover with the pastry lid, seal the edges and cover as described. Steam for 2½ hours. Run a sharp knife round the edge of the pudding and turn it out on to a heated serving dish. Serve with fresh or soured cream and soft brown sugar.

Serves 4

PUDDINGS

The ultimate ideal in economy is to cook a whole meal at the same time, in the same appliance and at the same temperature. I never have been able to bear the waste of switching on an oven for just one dish and so gradually I have built up a file of not-too-complicated puddings, listed under the oven temperatures they require. This way it is easy to flip through the ones that fit exactly into your oven scheme for the day.

Baked puddings don't all need to be stodge, though some of the nursery and family favourites are, admittedly, a bit on the heavy side.

If the casserole you are serving has a crumble or scone topping, go for a fruit-based pudding or one with a meringue texture that is light by contrast. Or bake one that will taste just as good cold, and have it waiting in the wings tomorrow.

And as with casserole dishes, consider the pudding recipes as a catalogue of variables. If the ingredients list calls for strawberries and it's redcurrants you have in surplus, substitute them. If the crumble calls for rhubarb and it's out of season or too expensive just now, use plums, or apples or dried apricots. After all, it is by just this kind of mix and match that new recipes are born, and new recipe books written!

Oven temperature 130°C–150°C (250°F–300°F)/Gas 1–2

Hazelnut Meringues

Decorative piped meringue cases can be filled with fresh soft fruit—raspberries and strawberries are ideal, of course—with stiff fruit purée or whipped cream folded with chopped hazelnuts, stem ginger, or with a 'sharp' purée; redcurrant is very good.

4 egg whites	For the filling:
225 g (8 oz) caster sugar	*150 ml (¼ pint) redcurrant purée,*
50 g (2 oz) shelled hazelnuts,	*slightly sweetened*
ground	*150 ml (¼ pint) double cream, whipped*
	150 ml (¼ pint) single cream, to serve

Whisk the egg whites until they are stiff and dry. Sprinkle on 1 tablespoon of the sugar and whisk again until thick, then whisk in the remaining sugar, a tablespoon at a time. When the mixture is dry, fold in the ground hazelnuts, using a metal spoon.

Very lightly brush sheets of greaseproof paper with oil, or use non-stick paper, and line 2 baking sheets. Fit a large star icing nozzle into a piping bag, two-thirds fill it with meringue mixture and pipe 12 'solid' circles about 10 cm (4 in) in diameter. Pipe an extra rim round each circle, to make the sides of the basket, and finish off with a star of the mixture at the join. Bake the meringue baskets at 130°C (250°F)/Gas 1, for at least 2 hours until they are thoroughly dry. Cool them on a wire rack. Store in an airtight container until you need them.

To make the filling, stir the fruit purée into the whipped cream and pile it into each basket. Serve with single cream.

Makes 12 baskets

Pineapple Pavlova

People who aren't always lucky with meringues—yes, there are those of us whose meringues 'weep' every so often—can gain confidence and compliments by making pavlova. It's a marvellous marshmallowy meringue texture; and 'touch wood', I've never known it to go wrong.

3 egg whites	For the filling:
175 g (6 oz) caster sugar	*1 450-g (16-oz) can pineapple*
2 teaspoons cornflour	*chunks, drained*
1 teaspoon lemon juice or distilled	*150 ml (¼ pint) double cream,*
vinegar	*whipped*
½ teaspoon vanilla essence	*sprigs of mint to garnish*

Whisk the egg whites until they are very stiff. Beat in half the sugar, and whisk until the mixture is stiff again. Using a metal spoon, fold in the remaining sugar, the cornflour, lemon juice or vinegar and vanilla essence.

Lightly brush 2 sheets of greaseproof paper with oil, or use non-stick paper, and line 2 baking sheets. Fit a plain nozzle inside a piping bag and two-thirds fill the bag with the mixture. Pipe 12 'solid' circles with 7·5-cm (3-in) diameters. Bake at 145°C (290°F)/Gas 1½, for ½ hour, reduce the heat to 135°C (265°F)/Gas ¾, and bake for a further ½ hour. The pavlova cases should be crisp and golden on the outside and soft on the inside. Cool the cases on wire racks, then peel off the paper. Store them in an airtight container until you need them.

Reserve a few pieces of pineapple for decoration and stir the remainder into the whipped cream. Just before serving, spread 4 pavlova circles with cream, cover each one with another circle, more cream, then a third circle. Spread the remaining cream on top of the 4 pavlova 'sandwiches', and decorate with the reserved pineapple and sprigs of mint.

Serves 4

Danish Orange Meringue

The advantage of this method of making soft meringue is that you bake it for an hour, switch off the heat, and complete the cooking as the oven cools— free.

1 teaspoon cornflour
1 teaspoon vanilla essence
1 teaspoon distilled vinegar
3 egg whites
200 g (7 oz) caster sugar

For the filling:
50 g (2 oz) butter, softened
100 g (4 oz) icing sugar, sifted
grated rind of 1 orange
1 teaspoon orange juice
150 ml (¼ pint) double cream, whipped
350 g (12 oz) fresh raspberries
extra caster sugar to decorate

Mix together the cornflour, vanilla essence and vinegar. Whisk the egg whites until stiff, whisk in 1 tablespoon of the sugar and continue whisking until the mixture is stiff and dry. Fold in the remaining sugar and the cornflour mixture, using a metal spoon. Cover a baking sheet with oiled greaseproof paper or non-stick paper and sprinkle it with caster sugar. Tip the meringue mixture on to the paper and spread it to a circle about 3 cm (1½ in) thick. Cook at 140°C (275°F)/Gas 1 for 1 hour, switch off the oven and leave the meringue to cool for an hour. (If your oven cools immediately on switching off, leave the meringue at the very lowest setting for the extra hour.) Leave the meringue on a wire rack until thoroughly cool, then tear off the paper.

To make the filling, beat the butter and icing sugar together, add the grated orange rind and beat in the orange juice. Fold the whipped cream into the butter cream and, just before serving, pile it into the meringue case. Cover the top of the cream with raspberries and dredge with extra caster sugar.

Serves 6

Oven temperature 180°C (350°F)/Gas 4

Almond Apples

Apples stuffed with marzipan for a true almond flavour can be served with a creamy, caramel-tasting sauce to make them high-days and holiday fare.

8 large cooking apples, cored
100 g (4 oz) marzipan
8 dates, stoned
50 g (2 oz) butter, melted

For the sauce (optional):
100 g (4 oz) butter

50 g (2 oz) black treacle
225 g (8 oz) soft dark brown sugar
½ teaspoon ground cinnamon
300 ml (½ pint) single cream
grated rind and strained juice of 1 lemon

Stand the apples in a shallow ovenproof dish or a roasting pan. Pack the cavities with marzipan as far as the centre, push a date in each and fill to the top of the fruit with marzipan. Brush the apples with the melted butter and bake at 180°C (350°F)/Gas 4, for 45 minutes.

To make the sauce, dissolve the butter, treacle, sugar and cinnamon in a small pan. Add the cream with the lemon rind and juice and bring to the boil. Simmer for 4 minutes, stirring from time to time. Pour the sauce over the apples to serve.

Serves 4

Orange Sunflowers *(photograph facing page 133)*

These are real party-pieces, oranges with strips of rind folded back like petals and their centres filled with dried fruit, like pollen.

4 large oranges
50 g (2 oz) seedless raisins (chop large ones)
50 g (2 oz) shelled hazelnuts or blanched almonds, chopped

4 tablespoons clear honey
1 tablespoon dark rum (optional)
2 teaspoons lemon juice
2 tablespoons water

With a very sharp knife, pare the orange rinds down into 8 segments, without cutting right through to the bottom. Carefully cut between the segments of the orange and, using a finger, gently open them out to leave a hole in the centre. Fill the centre hole with a mixture of the raisins and nuts. Carefully pull down each strip of orange rind, tucking the top point of each strip between the rind and the orange—the strips of rind then form loops, with the rind on the outside and the pith on the inside.

Cut 4 squares of household foil large enough to enfold the oranges and butter them well. Place an orange in the centre of each. In a small pan, heat together the honey, rum if used, lemon juice and water until the honey has dissolved. Spoon the mixture over the oranges and fold the foil to enclose the fruit completely. Place the foil parcels on a baking sheet and bake at 180°C (350°F)/Gas 4, for 15 minutes. Unwrap the foil, and serve the orange sunflowers with whipped cream or ice cream.

Serves 4

Caramel Pears

Anyone who has cooking-pear trees knows the problem of trying to serve the fruit in dozens of different, delicious ways—at least, I do. This way, with a spicy, tangy sauce, is so simple it almost feels like cheating.

4 large, firm pears
8 tablespoons clear honey
50 g (2 oz) butter, melted

2 tablespoons lemon juice
½ teaspoon ground cinnamon

Peel the pears but leave the stalks intact. Stand the pears upright in a fireproof dish. Mix together the honey, melted butter, lemon juice and cinnamon and spoon over the pears. Bake at 180°C (350°F)/Gas 4, for 20–30 minutes, until the sauce is a deep mid-brown. Serve hot or cold, with fresh soured cream.

Serves 4

Gooseberry Custard Pudding

Make use of the lower oven shelf to soften the fruit, then bring the dish to the top to bake the custard. A casserole cooking at the same time will be quite amenable to changing places!

450 g (1 lb) gooseberries, topped
* and tailed*
150 g (6 oz) caster sugar
2 eggs

2 150-ml (¼-pint) cartons fresh
* soured cream*
1 tablespoon flour
soft light brown sugar to serve

Put the gooseberries in a shallow ovenproof dish with half the sugar and cook at 180°C (350°F)/Gas 4 until the fruit begins to soften and turn yellow— about ½ hour. Beat the eggs, soured cream and flour together with the rest of the sugar and pour over the fruit. Bake for a further 45 minutes until the custard has risen like a soufflé and is golden brown on top. Strew with soft brown sugar and serve at once, before the custard subsides.

Serves 4

Tipsy Bread and Butter Pudding

Here is a recipe that neither nanny nor mother would have served in the nursery. Most men actually agree that the addition of rum is an improvement!

8 small slices fruit bread, buttered	*3 eggs*
50 g (2 oz) sultanas	*25 g (1 oz) caster sugar*
50 g (2 oz) mixed candied peel,	*2 tablespoons dark rum*
finely chopped	*25 g (1 oz) grated chocolate to*
450 ml (¾ pint) milk	*decorate*

Cut the crusts from the bread and arrange it in layers with the dried fruit and peel in a well-buttered baking dish or casserole. Beat together the milk, eggs, caster sugar and rum and pour over the dish. Allow to stand for ½ hour, then stand the dish in a larger one containing a little cold water. This will prevent the bottom of the pudding browning too quickly. Bake at 180°C (350°F)/ Gas 4, for 45 minutes until the top is golden brown. Sprinkle the grated chocolate on top as soon as you remove the pudding from the oven. Serve warm.

Serves 4

Crunchy Lemon Meringue

A lemon meringue pie with a difference—the crust is made of crisped-up bread. It's a good way to hide any slight error in over-ordering at the baker's!

2 teaspoons caster sugar	*50 g (2 oz) sugar*
75 g (3 oz) butter	*grated rind and strained juice of 1*
6 slices white bread, cut from a large	*large lemon*
loaf	*2 egg yolks*

For the filling:	For the meringue:
2 tablespoons cornflour	*2 egg whites*
300 ml (½ pint) water	*75 g (3 oz) caster sugar*

Beat the sugar into the butter. Cut the crusts from the bread and spread both sides with the sweetened butter. Cut 5 of the slices into 3 fingers and arrange them close together round the sides of a deep 1·5-litre (2½-pint) ovenproof dish, with the whole slice in the bottom. Bake at 180°C (350°F)/Gas 4, for 20 minutes, until the 'pie crust' is crisp.

To make the filling, blend the cornflour with 3 tablespoons of the water. In a small pan, bring to the boil the rest of the water, the sugar, lemon rind and juice. Stir in the blended cornflour and cook to thicken. Remove from the heat and leave to cool slightly. Whisk in the egg yolks one at a time, return the pan to a low heat and cook, stirring, for 1 minute. Remove the pan from the heat.

To make the meringue, whisk the egg whites until stiff and gradually add the sugar, whisking between each addition.

Pour the lemon mixture into the pie case and pile the meringue on top. Bake for a further 5–10 minutes until the top is golden brown. Serve hot.

Serves 4–6

Apple Cake

There are apple cakes to serve cold for tea and others, like this one, to serve hot as a pudding. I like them all; they are an ideal way to use purée from the freezer.

175 g (6 oz) butter	*450 ml (¾ pint) apple purée,*
175 g (6 oz) caster sugar	*sweetened*
3 eggs, beaten	*1 tablespoon mixed candied peel,*
175 g (6 oz) self-raising flour	*chopped*
¼ teaspoon mixed spice	*1 tablespoon granulated sugar to*
¼ teaspoon ground cinnamon	*decorate*

Beat together the butter and caster sugar until light and creamy and add a little of the beaten eggs. Sift together the flour, spice and cinnamon and add alternately with the rest of the egg. Stir in the apple purée and chopped peel. Turn the mixture into a greased 1·5-litre (2½-pint) ovenproof dish and bake at 180°C (350°F)/Gas 4, for 20–25 minutes, until golden brown. Sprinkle while still hot with the granulated sugar and serve with whipped cream.

Serves 6

Pear Gingerbread

Canned pears take well to a little gingering up. Here, it's a moist gingerbread that forms the base for pears cooked in a honey sauce.

75 g (3 oz) margarine	1 egg
75 g (3 oz) clear honey	150 g (5 oz) flour
1 400-g (15-oz) can pears, drained	½ teaspoon baking soda
few pieces stem ginger, drained	3 teaspoons ground ginger
50 g (2 oz) golden syrup	150 ml (¼ pint) milk
40 g (1½ oz) sugar	pinch of salt

Grease the sides of an 18-cm (7-in) cake tin. In a small pan, melt one-third of the margarine and all the honey and pour into the base of the tin. Cut the pears in half lengthwise and arrange, flat side down, in the tin, with a slice of stem ginger in the centre of each. Cream the remaining margarine, the syrup and sugar together and beat in the egg. Sift together the flour, baking soda and ground ginger and fold into the syrup mixture, adding enough milk to make a thick batter. Pour over the pears and bake at 180°C (350°F)/Gas 4, for about 40 minutes, until the centre feels firm to the touch. Turn out on to a shallow serving dish and serve hot or cold.

Serves 4

Blackcurrant Cake

When soft fruit is scarce, or expensive, or both, we have to turn to recipes that make a little go a long way. This one, with blackcurrants folded into the cake mixture, is rich and gorgeous.

100 g (4 oz) butter	little milk
100 g (4 oz) caster sugar	100 g (4 oz) blackcurrants, topped
2 eggs	and tailed (or use frozen ones,
175 g (6 oz) self-raising flour	thawed, or canned ones, drained)
½ teaspoon ground cinnamon	

Grease and line a 20-cm (8-in) cake tin.

Cream together the butter and sugar until light and fluffy, then beat in the eggs one at a time, adding a tablespoon of flour with each. Fold in the rest of the flour with the cinnamon and add a little milk if necessary to make a soft dropping consistency. Stir in the prepared blackcurrants. Bake at 180°C (350°F)/Gas 4, for 40 minutes, until the cake is firm to the touch. Turn out on to a large plate. Serve hot with whipped cream. It is also good cold.

Serves 4–6

Almond Apricot Pudding

Fruit at the bottom, sponge cake on top, is a popular pudding. This one, gooey with dried apricots and topped with browned almonds, is as good as any.

225 g (½ lb) dried apricots, soaked
  overnight
50 g (2 oz) soft light brown sugar
75 g (3 oz) butter
75 g (3 oz) caster sugar

½ teaspoon almond essence
2 eggs, separated
100 g (4 oz) self-raising flour
25 g (1 oz) blanched almonds, flaked

Drain the soaked apricots and put them in a greased 1·2-litre (2-pint) ovenproof dish. Sprinkle them with the brown sugar. Cream together the butter and caster sugar until light and fluffy and beat in the almond essence and egg yolks. Fold in the flour. Whisk the egg whites until they are stiff and fold into the sponge mixture. Spread over the fruit and sprinkle the flaked almonds on top. Bake at 180°C (350°F)/Gas 4, for 45–50 minutes.

Serves 4–5

Lemon Surprise

In some recipes, if the lemon juice you had carefully mixed into the other ingredients separated and sank to the bottom, it would be a disaster. In this one, it's a pleasant surprise, producing a melting lemony sauce.

25 g (1 oz) butter
75 g (3 oz) caster sugar
2 eggs, separated

grated rind and juice of 1 lemon
40 g (1½ oz) self-raising flour
150 ml (¼ pint) milk

Cream the butter and sugar together until light and fluffy and beat in the egg yolks. Mix in the lemon rind and juice, flour and milk. Whisk the egg whites until stiff and fold into the mixture. Pour into a greased 900-ml (1½-pint) ovenproof dish and bake at 180°C (350°F)/Gas 4, for 40–45 minutes. Make sure everyone has their share of the lemon sauce!

Serves 4

Spice Biscuits

It's useful to pop a tray of biscuits into the oven while a casserole is cooking (put the biscuits on the top shelf). These Dutch ones are super with an old-fashioned creamy pudding such as syllabub or posset.

75 g (3 oz) butter
65 g (2¼ oz) soft light brown sugar
115 g (4½ oz) self-raising flour
pinch of salt
¼ teaspoon mixed spice
½ teaspoon ground cinnamon

grated rind of ½ lemon
50 g (2 oz) blanched almonds,
  chopped
15 g (½ oz) digestive biscuits,
  crushed
caster sugar to decorate

Cream together the butter and sugar until light and fluffy. Sieve the flour, salt and spices and work into the butter mixture with the lemon rind, almonds and biscuit crumbs. Knead the dough until it is smooth and free of cracks. Roll the mixture on a very lightly-floured board to a thickness of $\frac{1}{4}$ cm ($\frac{1}{8}$ in), and cut into fancy shapes with biscuit cutters. Re-roll the trimmings and cut out again. Place the biscuits on a greased baking sheet and bake at 180°C (350°F)/Gas 4, for 10–12 minutes, until they are golden brown. Cool on a wire rack and lightly sprinkle with caster sugar before serving.

Makes about 36 biscuits

Oven temperature 190°C (375°F)/Gas 5

Coconut Spongies

Sometimes it makes a change to pass round a dish of cakes or cookies instead of serving a pudding. These are especially popular with children.

100 g (4 oz) butter	*1 tablespoon instant coffee powder*
50 g (2 oz) soft light brown sugar	*few drops of vanilla essence*
1 tablespoon clear honey	*75 g (3 oz) desiccated coconut*
100 g (4 oz) flour	

Cream together the butter and sugar until light and fluffy and beat in the honey. Sift the flour and coffee powder on to the mixture and fold it in. Stir in the vanilla essence and beat well. Form the mixture into small balls and roll them in the coconut. Place on a greased baking sheet and bake at 190°C (375°F)/Gas 5 for 10–15 minutes, until firm. Cool on a wire rack. To achieve a more nutty finish, brush the balls with more honey and roll them in coconut again.

Date and Rhubarb Crumble

I can never resist the crumble puddings they serve in some health-food restaurants; and can never resist trying to find new combinations of fruit to hide under the wholemeal topping.

450 g (1 lb) rhubarb, trimmed and cut into 2·5-cm (1-in) pieces	*2 bananas, peeled and thinly sliced*
75 g (3 oz) stoneless dates, roughly chopped	*100 g (4 oz) wholemeal flour*
50 g (2 oz) soft dark brown sugar	*50 g (2 oz) butter*
	50 g (2 oz) demerara sugar

Put the rhubarb, dates and sugar into a greased 1·2-litre (2-pint) ovenproof dish and mix well. Completely cover the top with sliced banana. (This not only tastes delicious, but stops the crumble trickling into the fruit.) Rub the flour and butter together and stir in the sugar. Sprinkle on the banana and bake at 190°C (375°F)/Gas 5, for 45 minutes. Serve hot with fresh soured cream.

You can substitute apples for the rhubarb when it is out of season.

Serves 4

Evesham Crumble

This is a type of crumble, made more nutty by the addition of oatmeal to the topping.

450 g (1 lb) greengages	*½ teaspoon cinnamon*
75 g (3 oz) sugar	*75 g (3 oz) oatmeal*
1 tablespoon water	*75 g (3 oz) butter*
50 g (2 oz) wholemeal flour	*50 g (2 oz) soft light brown sugar*

Put the greengages in an ovenproof dish and sprinkle them with sugar and water. Sift together the flour and cinnamon and mix in the oatmeal. Rub in the butter and stir in the brown sugar. Sprinkle the crumble mixture over the fruit and bake at 190°C (375°F)/Gas 5, for 45 minutes, when the fruit should be cooked and the topping crisp. Serve hot with whipped cream.

Serves 4–6

Oven temperature 200°C (400°F)/Gas 6

Dutch Fritters

The yeast in these fritters makes them rise quickly and, for you, effortlessly. They are also good served with plain stewed fruit.

225 g (8 oz) flour	*300 ml (½ pint) milk, warm*
pinch of salt	*50 g (2 oz) caster sugar*
1 teaspoon sugar	*50 g (2 oz) butter*
15 g (½ oz) dried yeast	

Sieve the flour and salt into a bowl and add the sugar. Dissolve the yeast in the warm milk and pour on to the flour. Mix well to form a soft dough. Pour the mixture into hot greased patty tins and bake at 200°C (400°F)/Gas 6, for 10 minutes. Dredge with caster sugar. Serve with melted butter and warmed maple syrup, treacle or honey.

Serves 4

Country Cobbler *(photograph facing page 133)*

Scone topping is a marvellous one-pot idea for casseroles. It's good with fruit, too. Try it with plums, greengages, apricots, rhubarb, all the favourite hot-pudding fruits.

900 g (2 lb) cooking apples, peeled, cored and sliced
4 tablespoons water
100 g (4 oz) soft light brown sugar
pinch of powdered clove

For the topping:
225 g (8 oz) self-raising flour
pinch of salt
75 g (3 oz) butter
15 g ($\frac{1}{2}$ oz) caster sugar
2 eggs, beaten
$\frac{1}{2}$ teaspoon cinnamon
2 tablespoons golden syrup

Put the apples with the water, brown sugar and powdered clove in an ovenproof dish and soften for 20 minutes in a warm oven.

To make the topping, sift flour and salt together, rub in the butter and stir in the caster sugar. Mix in the beaten eggs, using a spatula or round-bladed knife. Mix to form a smooth dough. Break off pieces of the dough, shape into balls and arrange on top of the hot fruit. Sprinkle the top lightly with cinnamon and dribble the syrup over. Bake at 200°C (400°F)/Gas 6, for 20 minutes until the cobbler topping has risen and is golden brown. Serve hot with single cream.

Serves 6

Strawberry Choux Buns

When the oven is at this temperature for another dish, it's a good opportunity to puff up some choux buns. They will keep perfectly for a day or two in an airtight container. Fill them just before serving.

150 ml ($\frac{1}{4}$ pint) water
50 g (2 oz) butter
65 g (2$\frac{1}{2}$ oz) flour, sifted
2 eggs

For the filling:
225 g (8 oz) fresh strawberries or other soft fruit, hulled
150 ml ($\frac{1}{4}$ pint) double cream, lightly whipped
icing sugar, sifted, to decorate

Put the water and butter in a small pan and bring to the boil. Remove from the heat and beat in the sifted flour. Return to the heat and cook for 2–3 minutes, beating with a wooden spoon. The mixture should leave the sides of the pan and form a ball. Allow to cool slightly and beat in the eggs one at a time. Put 6 spoonfuls of the mixture, well spaced out, on to a greased baking tray. Bake at 200°C (400°F)/Gas 6, for 30–35 minutes, until the buns are well risen and hollow. Remove the tray from the oven, split each bun through one side and cool on a wire rack.

Lightly stir the strawberries into the cream and fill the buns just before serving. Sift some icing sugar over to decorate.

Serves 6

Oven temperature 220°C (425°F)/Gas 7

Real Treacle Tart

Notice how everyone goes for the treacle tart if it's one of several puddings on offer at a party. This recipe is the best I know.

short-crust pastry made with 175 g (6 oz) flour etc (see page 73)
75 g (3 oz) fresh white breadcrumbs
25 g (1 oz) mixed candied peel, chopped
75 g (3 oz) sultanas
75 g (3 oz) currants
grated rind and strained juice of 1 lemon
1 apple, peeled, cored and grated
2 teaspoons ground cinnamon
1 teaspoon mixed spice
4 tablespoons black treacle
25 g (1 oz) butter, melted

Roll out the pastry and line a greased deep 20-cm (8-in) flan case. Roll over the edges to trim and prick all over the base with a fork. Combine the remaining ingredients and pour into the pie shell. Bake at 220°C (425°F)/ Gas 7, for 10 minutes. Reduce the heat to 190°C (375°F)/Gas 5, and cook for a further 20–25 minutes. Serve warm with single cream.

Serves 6–8

Index